An Introduction To Catholic Sacramental Theology

An Introduction To Catholic Sacramental Theology

Alexandre Ganoczy

Translated by
Reverend William Thomas

with the assistance of
Reverend Anthony Sherman

Paulist Press *New York/Ramsey*

Originally published under the title *Einfuhrung in die katholische Sakramentenlehre* from *Die Theologie: Einfuhrungen in Gegenstand, Methoden und Ergebnisse ihrer Disziplinen und Nachbarwissenschaften,* copyright © 1979 by Wissenschaftliche Buchgesellschaft, Darmstadt/Germany. English translation copyright © 1984 by The Missionary Society of St. Paul the Apostle in the State of New York.

Library of Congress
Catalog Card Number: 83-62461

ISBN: 0-8091-2568-4

Published by Paulist Press
545 Island Road, Ramsey, New Jersey 07446

Printed and bound in the United States of America

CONTENTS

ABOUT THE AUTHOR

Dr. Alexandre Ganoczy was born in Budapest, Hungary, in 1928. He has earned doctoral degrees in theology and philosophy. From 1966 to 1971 he was lecturer in the theological faculty of the Institut Catholique, Paris, and at the University of Munster, in West Germany. Since 1972, Dr. Ganoczy has been professor for dogmatic theology at the University of Wurzburg, West Germany. He has been involved in Calvin research, receiving grants from the Centre National de la Recherche Scientifique (1966-1971) and the Deutsche Forschungsgemeinschaft (since 1973), has published numerous books, among which are: *Calvin, theologien de l'Eglise et du ministere* (1964), *Le jeune Calvin* (1966), *Ecclesia ministrans, Dienende Kirche und kirchlicher Dienst bei Calvin* (1968), *Devenir chretien* (1973), *Sprechen von Gott in heutiger Gesellschaft* (1974), and *Der schopferische Mensch und die Schopfung Gottes* (1976). Prof. Ganoczy is also (since 1969) a member of the editorial committee of the ecumenical periodical *Concilium*.

ABBREVIATIONS

LG   "Lumen gentium," Dogmatic Constitution on the Church

AG   "Ad gentes divinitus," Decree on the Church's Missionary Activity

GS   "Gaudium et spes," Pastoral Constitution on the Church in the Modern World

DV   "Dei verbum," Dogmatic Constitution on Divine Revelation

OE   "Orientalium ecclesiarum," Decree on the Catholic Eastern Churches

AA   "Apostolican actuositatem," Decree on the Apostolate of Lay People

PO   "Presbyterorum ordinis," Decree on the Ministry and Life of Priests

SC   "Sacrosanctum concilium," Constitution on the Sacred Liturgy

OT   "Optatam totius," Decree on the Training of Priests

GE   "Gravissimum educationis," Declaration on Christian Education

UR   "Unitatis redintegratio," Decree on Ecumenism

CD   "Christus Dominus," Decree on the Pastoral Office of Bishops in the Church

2. Other Texts

Kus   K. Rahner. *Kirche und Sakramente,* QD 10. Freiburg-Basel-Wien, 1950.

ChSG   E. Schillebeeckx. *Christus, Sakrament der Gottesbegegnung.* Mainz, 1960.

ThEu   A. Gerken. *Theologie der Eucharistie.* Munchen, 1973.

DS   H. Denzinger, A. Schonmetzer. *Enchiridion symbolorum definitionum et declarationum des rabus Fidei et morum.* Basel-Freiburg-Rome, 1976.

NR   J. Neuner, H. Roos. *Der Glaube der Kirche in den Urkunden der Lehrverkundigung.* Regensburg, 1975.

PL   J. P. Migne (publisher). *Patrologiae cursus completus, series latina.* Paris, 1844–1855, 221 vols.

PG   J. P. Migne (publisher). *Patrologiae cursus completus, series graeca.* Paris, 1857-1866, 161 vols.

LThK   *Lexikon fur Theologie und Kirche.* Published by J. Hofer and K. Rahner. Freiburg, 1957-1967, 10 vols.; supplementary volumes, *LThK-K,* Second Vatican Council. Documents and commentaries, 3 vols., published by *op. cit.,* 1966-1968.

RGG   *Die Religion in Geschichte und Gegenwart. Handworterbuch fur Theologie und Religionswissenschaft.* Published by K. Galling. Tubingen, 1957-1965, 6 vols.

ThWNT   *Theologisches Worterbuch zum NT.* Founded by G. Kittel, published by G. Friedrich. Stuttgart, 1933-1973, 9 vols.

ThQ   *Theologische Quartalschrift.* Tubingen, 1819 ff.

ZNW   *Zeitschrift fur die neutestamentliche Wissenschaft und die Kunde der alteren Kirche.* Giessen, 1900 ff., Berlin 1934 ff.

GuL   *Geist und Leben. Zeitschrift fur Aszese und Mystik.* Wurzburg, 1947 ff. (before 1947 *ZAM,* Wurzburg, 1926 ff.)

WA   M. Luther. *Werke. Kritische Gesamtausgabe* (Weimarer Ausgabe). Weimar, 1883 ff.

INTRODUCTION

The purpose of this book is to enable the reader to approach Catholic sacramental teaching in both its historical and its contemporary setting. Taking into consideration the needs of students of theology as well as other interested readers, I wish not only to give an introduction to the dogmatic tradition but also to create an awareness of the important problems involved in this tradition. Explanation and critical comment must go hand in hand; the nature of the material demands it. Seen historically, both the theological discussion about the Church's teaching office and ecclesial practice concerning Christian cultic celebration were always accompanied by a lively tension between what had always been believed and newly raised questions and insights. The background understanding of the New Testament authors certainly provided the basic orientation for the entire tradition, but among the theologians of later times—Tertullian, Augustine, Thomas Aquinas, and the Council fathers of Trent and Vatican II—each explained, accentuated and worked with a comprehensive theory of the sacraments in his own way.

Catholic sacramental teaching and practice of the Middle Ages found itself suddenly in a crisis as a result of criticisms made by the Reformers. This crisis had a central importance for sacramental history because it challenged the teaching office of the Church to an extraordinarily fruitful clarification process which resulted in the texts of the Council of Trent on both sacraments in general and the seven individual sacraments in particular. The effectiveness of these documents has proven to be extensive. Yet, the systematic accomplishment of Trent was strongly influenced by an anti-Protestant defensiveness, and this has had a declining relevance over the last few decades. At the same time contemporary Catholic theology is influenced by the results of modern interconfessional exegesis. Thus there needs to be a comprehensive and constructive rethinking of the whole subject. This book especially acknowledges this important task by confirming the determinative role that the latest ecumenical Council gave to concrete expression of Church, liturgy and living witness in the world.

We can formulate the question which has confronted both the pre-conciliar and the post-conciliar Church in the following manner: How do sacraments function when both the concern which gave rise to them and the later conditions imposed by the experience and interpretation of those who have received them are taken into account? Such an interest stems from the level of personal understanding and must be included in this study so that it will be not only an introduction to current materials but will also treat concepts still in the process of becoming.

In Chapter One the term *sacrament* will be explained, keeping in mind its origins in the history of culture and religion. Its original form is to be found in the Greek concept of *mysterion*, an idea also used by the biblical authors. We will also treat under what circumstances this concept can be further transmitted by the Latin term *sacramentum* and how theologians, with their various systems of thought, have used this concept in their theories of Christian cultic practice. The main witnesses for this theological development will be Tertullian, Augustine, and Thomas Aquinas, as well as the Reformers, with their critical questioning of tradition. Didactically—for this belongs to our stated goals as well—this first chapter is designed to awaken an understanding of the complexity of our material in its historical development: how cultic, cultural, and philosophical elements are assimilated into the genesis of a key concept in both its pre- and inner-Christian history and how this process results in a more or less radical change within the concept.

Chapter Two expands the examination of the history of concept and theory in regard to the systematic of our *fundamental question*. The question concerning the effectiveness, the institution, the administration and the communication of the sacraments, as well as why there are seven, will be considered as necessary to a fundamental historical approach. Special attention must be given to the unavoidable variations in each era which the fathers in the patristic period, the theology of the Middle Ages, the Reformation and the Council of Trent, as well as more recent Catholic research, have offered in answer to this question.

A critique especially of contemporary approaches is helpful in this respect. The biblical basis for sacramental teaching, in its totality, offers several criteria for the formation of a judgment. Among other things the question of the legitimacy of presenting a tract on "sacraments in general" will be raised even though such a tract seeks to justly clarify the fundamental questions of seven sacraments factually quite different from each other. The expected pedagogical achievement of this chapter would be the reader's comprehension of the "magnificence and misery" of *theological systems* and their development. Whenever aspects of the Christian faith—which in any respect cannot be completely grasped rationally—must be reduced to a "common denominator," tensions arise; this is a basic theological given.

Convinced that one can only be introduced to Catholic sacramental teaching in a factually correct way when *all the individual sacraments* are portrayed in their unmistakable individuality, we have made this the theme for our third chapter. To make more prominent the differences in accent, which exist between a confessionally apologetic approach and an interconfessional scriptural and contemporary approach to the sacraments, the texts of the Council of Trent and of the Second Vatican Council (with its representative group of theologians) will be placed in juxtaposition. In doing this, not only must the "personality" of each sacrament be presented, but also a classic example of the scope and limitation of the *new interpretations* of traditional teaching with regard to relevant ecclesiological and anthropological questions. In this relatively extensive third chapter it could be of didactic value that the reader become acquainted with the typical methodology and vocabulary of the teaching office in both the sixteenth and the twentieth century. Since a considerable number of texts are quoted at length, the material in this chapter may seem more demanding.

In Chapter Four a new approach will be offered (with hypothetical care) using "communications theory" terminology with a view to understanding the structure and foundation of the sacraments. This attempt was occasioned, in part, by reflection on the content of the Augustinian symbol theory, but more so by the understanding of modern existential-philosophical anthropology (K. Rahner and E. Schillebeeckx have made this contribution to the latest research), and above all by the approach of Vatican II, insofar as it approaches the sacraments from a primarily practical-theological view, which is therefore influenced by the humanities. It was not by chance that its very first proclamation was the Constitution on the Sacred Liturgy.

The possible lesson learned in these discussions might be the clarification of the necessary interdisciplinary character of the various branches of theology within itself and theology's relation to numerous non-theological sciences. Thus it seems that contemporary research in the field of Catholic sacramental teaching is headed in the direction of a modern form of theory-practice unity which possesses its origins in the struggle of the first Christian theologians with the novelty of the Gospel. This struggle was well documented in the New Testament.

An excess of *footnotes* and extensive scientific *bibliography* have been purposely avoided. *Quotations* and other references are generally from a small number of works—which, by the way, I recommend as worth reading for a deeper understanding of this introduction, and for a point of comparison with it. The titles of these works are referred to in abbreviated form (see the list of abbreviations) and, for the sake of simplicity, directly in the text. A more complete list of references and literature for further reading are to be found at the end of this volume.

The author does not wish at this point to neglect a word of thanks to his co-workers, above all to his assistant Dr. Johannes Schmid for his valuable contribution to the quality of the text and his critical comments, and to Mrs. Christa Schoor for the preparation of the final manuscript. Further I wish to thank Dr. Cornelius P. Mayer and Dr. Helmut Feld for their valuable suggestions.

Chapter One

THE CONCEPT OF SACRAMENT IN ITS HISTORICAL DEVELOPMENT

Both in its linguistic and theological history, the Christian concept of sacrament developed out of the pre-Christian mystery concept. Alone the observation that in the first Christian centuries the Latin word *sacramentum* was the most common translation of the Greek term *mysterion* does not suffice to explain the unusually rich religious conceptual complex to which both words belong. For this it is necessary to examine both terms in their own historical context.

1.1. *Mysterion* in Cult and Philosophy

When the average person in our modern industrial society speaks of something "mysterious," he refers primarily to something puzzling, hidden, incomprehensible, strange—to something that can fascinate him for a time, but that does not concern him at a deeper level. In contrast to this, people of classical antiquity tended to see in mystery something existentially definitive which touched the very foundation of being and raised the sphere of human existence to that of the divine.

The classical concept of mystery manifests itself in two particular areas, the one cult and the other philosophy, whereby the former was the primary in point of time. This concept contained already much of what was later to become a part of the Christian discussion concerning sacraments.

1.1.1. Mystery in Cult

The plural form *mysteria* designated, since the seventh century B.C., primarily a whole group of secret cults that had developed among the Greeks (Eleusis, Dionysius, Orpheus, Samothrace), and in the Hellenic Orient (Adonis, Attis and Cybele, Isis and Osiris, Mithras), usually on the periphery of the commonly practiced religions. (Cf. K. Prumm, "Mysterien," in *LThK,* Vol. 7, pp. 717–720.) These "mysteries" developed almost exclusively from ancient fertility cults. Their goal was the increase or the restoration of vitality. They were celebrated in that the story of a divinity or of a divine couple was ritually reenacted within the circle of the already initiated. These celebrations communicated the experience of a divine drama in order to enable an actual participation in it (Bornkamm, p. 810). Was the apostle Paul consciously referring to such a conception when he said that through baptism the candidate dies with Christ and rises with Christ (cf Rom 6:4)? There are scholars who hold this position.[1]

Characteristic for the mystery cults was that only the consecrated and initiated were admitted to these celebrations. There were therefore rites of initiation by degrees into the fellowship of "mystics," as well as selected masters of these cults, the "hierophants" (esp. in Eleusis) and "mystagogues." These played, as it were, a priestly role. Whoever had been initiated enjoyed a brotherly solidarity with his co-mystics, was able to experience a security in their fellowship, and was at the same time strictly obliged to keep secret the particulars of the ritual. Whoever broke this obligation of secrecy, the so-called "arcanum," was considered guilty of sacrilege.

Only for the loyal was salvation (as in Christianity called *soteria)* promised or secure. Herein was the most profound root of their isolation from the mass of the initiated. They alone were privileged to have complete community of life with the divine precursors, beyond all suffering and death. They alone entered into the discipleship of the gods, who were themselves "redeemed saviors" moving in the polarity between life and death. However, the claim that the faith of Christians in their crucified Lord and in their communion with him in baptism and the Eucharist could be a variation of this mystery concept has been rejected by scholars. The gods of the mystery cults did not offer themselves freely for the whole world. They are themselves subject to a higher fate, whose dictates they suffer. They are subjected to the law of change, which, through their mediation, regulates the cosmic powers of death and rebirth (Bornkamm, p. 812). Here is to be seen the cyclical concept of the Greeks, their nature philosophy of the "eternal return of the same," which is decidedly opposed to the Jewish understanding of history as the possibility of creating the absolutely new.

Still the mystery cults sought a salvation that, in like manner, guaranteed an on-going development of life, both before and after death. Already in the present life the initiated experienced a communication of divine life-force; they called this (as did the Gnostics of their "illumination" and the Christians of their baptism) "new birth." And as reborn, they hoped for a hereafter where they would be granted, as the gods before them, "to pass through Hades without being destroyed" (Bornkamm, p. 813).

1.1.2. Mystery in Philosophy

Probably it was the great existential importance of the mystery cults that caused the classical Greek philosophers to liken their own efforts on the path toward the understanding of truth to the steps of the mystics on their path to initiation. We find such figures of speech especially with Plato. In his book *Symposion,* the female character of Diotima appears in the role of a hierophant; she leads the seeking philosopher to a vision of pure being (*Symp.* 210a–212c; cf *Phaedr.* 249a–250c). This leading, this ascension from the visible, changing world of objects to the invisible, unchanging world of reality (which for Plato is the only true reality) takes on the form of a mystery initiation, of a "mystagogy." The goal is of course beyond the cultic. It is epistemological and metaphysical. For Plato and the Platonists, it is a matter of that wisdom *(sophia),* which is able, in the visible objects of space and time, to comprehend the shadowy contours of the invisible One, Good, and Beautiful, and which is conscious of the symbolic, integrating function of the objects of world and nature. In the Platonic world-view, everything tangible becomes a *symbol* of the only truly real, heavenly, and divine Reality. The language of these symbols can be heard, and their hidden reality can be comprehended only by those who take leave of the sphere of the profane and are initiated into the philosophic mysteries (*Theaet.* 156a).

Here the question is no longer one of the secret rituals of a salvific cult, but of the secret teaching of a truth-bringing Wisdom. Not a plurality of suffering and redeemed deities is the attracting force, but the alone Real in its unspeakable and incomprehensible reality. And it is not the anticipated and reenacted process of death and life, but the invisible, unchangeable Divine to which the knowing sage climbs on the ladder of the visible replicas.

The history of Christian neo-Platonism, from Origen to the Augustinian sacrament theorists of the Middle Ages and the Reformation, demonstrates that this philosophical tradition has been more or less critically assimilated by Christian thinkers, not least of all with regard to the so-called sacraments of initiation with their emphasis on the profession of faith.

In many respects, the pre-Christian Gnostics certainly demonstrated a hybrid form of the cultic and philosophical mystery traditions. Here the term *mysterion* stood for the redeeming communication between the heavenly proto-man and the "spiritual" man, the "pneumatic," who, through "rebirth," i.e., through a process of perception and assimilation, becomes a living and "perfect" replica of the redeemed Redeemer.[2]

In the context of our present analysis it could be further noted that already in the classical period the *mystagogic vocabulary* became a part of profane terminology. For example, sleep as a preliminary to "eternal sleep," human intimate relations, the secrets of the medical profession, and even secrecy of the mails were referred to by the term *mysterion* (cf Bornkamm, p. 817).

1.2. *Mysterion* as Biblical Term

1.2.1. For a right understanding of the Christian concept of mystery, it is important to note that already the Old Testament texts, which were written in the Hellenistic period (Wisdom, Daniel, Tobit, Sirach, 2 Maccabees), used the term *mysterion* more however in its philosophic or profane sense than that of the cultic. (Examples of its use in the profane sense: Tob 12:7, 11; Jdt 2:2; Sir 22:22; 27:16f, 21; 2 Mac 13:21.) Here we shall consider only two books with particularly rich theological content: Wisdom and Daniel.

Foundational is the statement in Wisdom 2:22 that the wicked "knew not the hidden counsels *(mysteria)* of God." This refers, of course, to the one, speaking God of Israel, Yahweh. He is the subject of the mysteries which are to be understood and which are completely hidden to the wicked— e.g., to such as follow pagan secret cults (14:15, 23; cf 12:5). Opposed to this, the mysteries of the one God are revealed to all who are open and seek after Wisdom, which is seen as a personified Mediatrix between God and man (cf 8:4). Wisdom reveals the divine secrets and is itself a secret which must be revealed—as later the case with the Logos in the Gospel of John. The just person must know her if he desires to know God. Therefore he attends to the words of the teacher of wisdom:

> Now what wisdom is, and how she came to be I shall re-
> late and I shall hide no secrets from you. But from the
> very beginning I shall search out and bring to light
> knowledge of her, nor shall I diverge from the truth
> (6:22).

Whoever speaks in this way understands himself as a servant of the revelation of the great Revealer, as proclaimer and teacher of the mysteries, whose goal is the immortality and salvation of those who are open to understanding (cf 8:13). All of this is clearly in imitation of the terminology of non-Jewish mystery cults—as was the case with the Platonists; still, a real and essential proximity to these mystery cults or to the Gnostic redemption myths cannot be shown (Bornkamm, p. 820).

In the Book of Daniel, a completely new motif appears, the "eschatological" *mysterion*. It consists in "what is to happen in days to come" (2:28), and that is to be revealed by God himself. For it is ultimately God alone who is able to unveil the secrets of the future (2:47); for this purpose he uses, by his own sovereign choice, such symbolic devices of mediation as dreams and "visions" (2:18f). What the final future of the world will bring is the subject of a "veiled pronouncement" (Bornkamm, p. 821), the unveiling of which only God himself, or a prophet, directed by his Spirit, is capable.

These thoughts characterize as well the texts of the so-called *apocalyptic literature* in which, however, the mysteries of the final phase of history are strongly objectified. The secret counsels of the Almighty are portrayed as objects already present in heaven; only the visionary, in the moment of ecstasy, has present access to them. Here can be seen a certain likeness to the concepts of the mystery cults and the Gnostics. There are however three differences for the writers of apocalyptic literature: (a) the idea of a single sovereign God is indispensable, (b) they do not hold to the divinizing of the human individual, and (c) their intention is to fathom the fate of the universe through the events of a cosmic revelation.

1.2.2. In those instances where the New Testament texts speak of *mysterion* they reveal most often an apocalyptic influence and have a strongly eschatological accent.

Characteristically, Mark 4:11 combines *mysterion* with the key concept of Jesus' eschatological proclamation, *basileia* (kingdom). Even though the statement, "To you the mystery of the reign of God *(basileia)* has been confided," can hardly be seen as an authentic word of Jesus,[3] we can assume that Jesus understood the reign of God in an apocalyptic sense—as suddenly coming from God, as the reality of grace which brings salvation, as open only to those who have faith.

For Paul—and this is something decisively new—the reality of grace is so closely identified with the person of Jesus Christ that, for him, *mysterion* is essentially the Christ-event itself. Paul himself wishes to know and proclaim no other "wisdom" than the apparent contradiction of wisdom in the Crucified. In him is comprehended the "mystery" of God (1 Cor 2:1f;[4] cf Col 2:2). The apparent connection with Jewish wisdom, and perhaps with the Hellenic philo-sophia, receives in this way a defiant, paradoxical, provocative character—the shameful execution of the man Jesus on the cross reveals itself as the only true wisdom, which God planned "before all ages for our glory" (1 Cor 2:7). This is the "mystery" that is unveiled by the Spirit of God (cf 1 Cor 2:10-15) and is to be proclaimed by the apostles as "administrators of the mysteries of God" (1 Cor 4:1; Eph 3:2f; Col 1:25f). It must be proclaimed in the face of the philosophical, religious, and political "rulers of this age" (1 Cor 2:6, 8), who are themselves searching for ever more glorious mysteries.

Pauline theology makes a decisive break with all tendencies toward an elitist isolation and a privatizing of the search for salvation typical for the mystery cults. His *mysterion* demands no "arcanic" secrecy. On the contrary, it is to be open, public, and available for all. It is a confession of faith, outwardly directed and apostolic. How could it be any

other than that, since the new wisdom in Christ is addressed
to all peoples of the world? Not only the Jews, but the
"Gentiles" as well are included, unified in the *ecclesia* of
Christ together with his elect people, as the author of
Ephesians (3:4f) clearly states. The universal breakthrough,
the "economy" of the Christ-mystery (i.e., the mystery of
God which is Christ—cf Col 1:27; 2:2) among the peoples,
assumes the following phases: the will of God to bring a
salvific unity (Eph 1:9f; 3:4f), the crucifixion and resurrection of Jesus as *the* revelation and *the* realization of this will,
apostolic (Eph 3:2f; Col 1:25f) and ecclesial (Eph 3:10f)
proclamation. These phases cannot be experienced by one's
earning it, either by philosophical reflection or by ritual
participation. God alone, as Creator of the universe, can
initiate into the mystery of his salvation (cf Eph 3:9). He does
this substantially through the word, which is proclaimed by
the various servants of Christ.

Are "sacramental words" included in this? The New
Testament does not preclude this possibility, even though
the word *mysterion* is nowhere used as a term for baptism or
of the Lord's Supper. It would appear at this point that a
desire to make a distinction with the Hellenistic mystery
cults is at work. The intention to work toward a differentiation between the encounter with God in the community of
faith, and the foundational level of proclamation by word
and deed, may here be determinative.

1.3. *Mysterion* in the Ancient Church

Eschatologically historical, Christologically centered,
and ecclesial-apostolic openness—these three characteristics must be considered normative for any further development of Christian theology. This is valid for the "primary"
area of the proclamation of word and deed as well as for the
"secondary" area of sacramental cult. ("Secondary" means
here simply "non-fundamental" for Christian existence;
"fundamental" is above all the speaking witness of life
which is expressed, among other ways, in sacramental cult.)

Whether this norm was always clearly seen in the ancient Church and in the later tradition of the theologians can be questioned in the light of the many culturally conditioned variations in teaching. Already in the first centuries, the apologetic and missionary situation of the Church resulted in a recourse of its theologians to the cultic as well as to the philosophical heritage of their Hellenistic surroundings. In addition to this came very soon the influence of Roman culture.

1.3.1. From the Apostles to Augustine

Among the theologians of the second century whose goal was an apologetic (i.e., an intellectual defense of the Christian faith against its Jewish, Hellenistic, and Gnostic challengers),[5] most prominent in their *mysterion* interpretation were Justin, Irenaeus, Clement of Alexandria, and Tertullian. They used this term, in the first instance, polemically as a description of the secret Hellenistic cults (e.g., Justin, *Apol.* I25. 27. 54. 66; II12 [*PG* 6, 365. 370f. 407-11. 427f]; Tertullian, *De Praescr. Haer.* 40 [*PL* 2, 54f]) or of the secret teachings of the Gnosis (e.g., Tertullian, *De anima* 18; *PL* 2, 677-680). Still, they used the term for *biblically* attested events insofar as they saw in them moments in which the divine plan of salvation was realized. This was particularly true for their proof against the Gnostics of the unity of both Testaments or covenants, of the Old and the New. In the sense of a Pauline Christ-centeredness and economy of fulfillment, the events and institutions of the Old Testament are seen as typological pre-proclamation, or even as an anticipation of the salvation reality which appeared in Christ, and in this sense they are referred to as *mysterion* (cf Justin, *Dial.* 24; 40; 44; 111 [*PG* 6, 258f; 561-564; 569-572; 732f]). Consistent with this, the term is also used to designate particular events in the earthly life of Jesus, especially his birth and crucifixion (Justin, *Apol.* I13; *Dial.* 74. 91; [*PG* 6, 345-348; 649-652; 692f]).

Next to this line of thought, which uses the *mysteria* as

polemical proof of salvation history, there is a more philosophical line, which appears to be nearer the Gnosis, at least with respect to its terminology. This trend developed primarily in the neo-Platonist school of the Alexandrians. Clement of Alexandria presents Christ as the great Mystagogue who progressively introduces or initiates into the "lesser" and "greater" mysteries of eternal truth (*Strom.* IV3, 1; IV 162, 3 [*PG* 8, 1215; 8, 1371]). The transmission of the greatest mysteries, with which Christian teachers are entrusted, can ensue only in a veiled, cryptic, and parabolic manner, in order that the treasury of truth remain guarded from profanation (*Strom.* V57, 2; VI 124, 6 *PG* 9, 87; 9, 347)—an interesting reintroduction of the old spirit of exclusivity and law of secrecy into Christianity which, in its New Testament phase, knew only the "open" mysteries of God.

Less dangerous were the efforts of those apologists who, like Justinian (*Apol.* I 66; *PG* 6, 472f) and Tertullian (*De Praescr. Haer.* 40; *PL* 2, 54f), began, initially borrowing from the mystery cults, to call *baptism* and the *Lord's Supper mysteria*. It was without doubt their intention to hold firmly to Christ, whose living reality was beyond all ritual, as foundational for proclamation, faith and ethics—even when they inquired as to the ritual presence of this same Christ for the believing person and community here and now. Indeed one can say with a high degree of probability that they were able to call *both* of these *mysterion* (for the first time *sacramentum* by Tertullian) only because they placed strong emphasis on the relationship between the salvation which had been created by Christ and its ritual expression in the contemporary community of faith. These terms were valid in the given cultural context as terms of religious communication. Should it not be possible for them to use these terms to designate the rites of baptism and the Eucharist in which Paul saw a veiled but nonetheless real participation of the faithful in the destiny, in the passion and saving work of their crucified, risen and glorified Lord? Should it not be possible for them to so designate that interactive and permanent relationship which Romans

6:6-8 refers to as a being "crucified with him" in baptism so that the one baptized might also "live with him," or that 1 Corinthians 10:17 formulates in this way: "Because the loaf of bread is one, we, many though we are, are one body, for we all partake of the one loaf"?

An epochal aspect entered Christian theology as the Greek term *mysterion* was translated by the Latin word *sacramentum*.[6] This occurred first in the African version of the Bible and in the European version referred to as the "Itala." It was a lawyer, Tertullian, the educated son of a Roman officer, who was able to combine this translation with a newly attempted theological interpretation, which could only serve to aid the reception of Christianity in the Roman cultural world.[7]

For the Romans, the term *sacramentum* had a double meaning: the taking of an *oath*, and the giving of a *monetary guarantee*. In both cases the Roman idea of self-obligation as an important component of morality is here present. In addition, the relationship of such acts of self-commitment to the practice of oath-taking in the mystery cults played an important role.

A Roman who took an oath of allegiance for military or civil service was well aware of the religious implications of this act. It had the character of a "sacratio,"[8] the dedicating of oneself to an authority which had divine character. In addition was the fact that oath-taking often was in the form of a consecration and included the entreating of powers from the underworld while excluding all the unworthy from these proceedings. And then the mystery cults themselves often combined their initiation rituals with an oath based on the military model of oaths of allegiance. The translation of *mysterion* with *sacramentum* recommends itself in a number of respects.

When a Roman was engaged in a legal conflict, he saw this as a sacral process. He knew that in certain cases only an appeal to the gods could determine someone's guilt, or the degree of his guilt. As a sign of his willingness to humble himself before the "divine judgment," every plaintiff brought a sum of money as security to the duly qualified priest; and this sum was then referred to as a *sacramentum.*

This pre-Christian use of the word makes the reason clear for Tertullian's use of the term primarily in reference to baptism (*Ad Martyros* 3, 1; *De spectaculis* 24, 4; *De corona* 11, 1; *Scorpiace* 4, 5; *De idolatria* 19, 2 [*PL* 1, 697; 1, 730f; 2, 91ff; 2, 129f; 1, 767f]). It refers, of course, to adult baptism. Herein the Roman soldier's son and lawyer saw the great free-will commitment of the converted pagan to the service of the one God and of the Lord Jesus Christ. The baptismal candidate committed himself by an oath to invest all of his energies for Christ—when necessary in martyrdom, but in any case to the testimony of a life filled with love.

Such self-commitment of the candidate was, for Tertullian, by no means a blind act of trust. He was confronted with a decision based on the clear testimony of faith-knowledge. The sacrament of baptism orients itself on content that is summed up in the creedal statement of the Church and thoroughly founded on the biblical revelation. So it is no wonder when the apologist saw the relevancy of the term *sacramentum* as extending to the *mysteria* of salvation history. The prophetic pre-proclamation, the ritual anticipation of salvation in Old Testament history, and naturally the fulfillment in the deeds of Jesus Christ are called *sacramenta.* They are a guarantee from God of the truths to which the baptismal candidate commits himself in his profession of faith.

It can be seen that already Tertullian presents what modern theologians might call "sacramental interaction" (cf 4.2.). Certainly that personal "yes" to the statement of faith, the faith through which the baptismal candidate places complete confidence in the revelation of his God, is sacramental. But God's offer is already sacramental. God offers in baptism a commitment to the faithful to adopt him as a son and to transform him into the likeness of his only begotten Son. We could also say that God proffers the biblically guaranteed *sacramenta* of his fatherly desire to save. The individual is to respond through the *sacramenta* of Christian ritual and so achieve an ethical and active correspondence. In this way God awakens activity, an activity of human response; the commitment, just as in the old covenant, is to be reciprocal. This commitment expresses itself as a sign of enlightenment and of substantiation; as guarantee for the promises which have already been fulfilled in Christ and which are the *sacramenta* of God that pre-date all ritual.

Tertullian did not, of course, develop all of these thoughts into such a systematic form. Still his understanding of *sacramentum* would seem to allow a systematizing of his approach as here given. There needs to be no extended argumentation to prove that his attempts in this direction not only served the apostolic extension of Christianity in the Roman imperium, but have also proved (and are proving) helpful for a modern reformulation of sacramental teaching.

This approach of Tertullian to baptism (and to some degree to the Eucharist), which was aimed at an active ethic and a strong discipline of faith, was not able to hold out long against the competition of an understanding of sacraments inspired by a mystical-Platonist approach. Even though the military symbolism is still evident in Cyprian and Arnobius, and sporadically in Ambrose, it began in the fourth century to disappear completely.[9] In place of this, a theology of sacraments spread in both East and West which must now be considered.

(a) The main interest now became the realization, the making present, of the saving deeds of Christ through ritual celebration, to make possible a participation in the essentials of salvation. There was no hesitation in referring to the historically unique events of the crucifixion and resurrection of Jesus as being "repeated in the mystery."[10]

(b) In this context the Eucharist as sacrifice comes to the fore. The self-sacrifice of Christ, symbolically and mystically veiled in the eucharistic sacrifice, is brought to remembrance and is made present for the benefit of the participants (cf Eusebius, *Demonstratio evangelica* I 10, 38; *PG* 22, 90). Occasionally the idea appears that Christ makes himself present (*op. cit.* V 3, 19; *PG* 22, 365).

(c) The Platonic double system of the original and the

copy (i.e., of *typos* and *antitypos*), was introduced to elucidate the mystery-presence of Christ's saving deeds. The Eucharist is a real re-presentation as "antitype" of the great "original" mysteries (Gregory of Nazianzus, *Or.* 2, 95; *PG* 35, 488A) of the life of Christ.

(d) In all of these assertions, the terminology of the mystery cults is increasingly evident from the fourth century on, terms such as consecration, perfection, initiation, imitation, and rebirth.[11]

1.3.2. Augustine

With Augustine there occurred a truly epochal turning point in Christian sacramental understanding. Using a neo-Platonist epistemology and ontology, he was able to construct a consistent and systematic theology of sacraments. While Tertullian determined everything from a standpoint of practical conduct, and Greek theologians spoke of baptism and the Eucharist in terms of the mystery cults, Augustine constructed a both philosophical and theological theory of sacramentality. In this way he enriched the dimension of ethical conduct and of ritual experience with that of a theoretical understanding.

Augustine wrote no tract concerning the mysteries or the sacraments as did, for example, his teacher Ambrose of Milan (*De mysteriis* [*PL* 16, 404-426]; *De sacramentis* [*PL* 16, 435-482]). Still his treatise *De magistro* (*PL* 32, 1193-1220) on signs, the "signa," is considered a fundamental theology of sacramentality in general. In this work the bishop of Hippo presents his neo-Platonist theory of symbols, on which his entire reflection on various objects, which he calls *sacramenta,* is based. *Sacramentum* is for him a specific species of the family of symbols belonging "to the divine things" and which has to do with the realm of the sacred.[12]

It is possible in the Augustinian symbol theory to systematically distinguish four levels—epistemology, its foundational ontology, a theological application, and the consequences for a specific theology of sacraments.

    (a) For the *epistemological level,* Augustine's following definition is of basic importance: "A sign is a thing that, apart from its appearance to the senses, causes something more to come to mind" (*De doctr. christ.* III 9, 13; *PL* 34, 70). The connection between the sign and that signified can be of a natural sort (e.g., between the smoke and the burning wood), or it can be determined by the free choice of an individual (e.g., the linguistic expression of a thought). In any case, a whole system of references crystallizes around each symbol. The symbol refers us to the signified, but the signified can itself become a symbol for further points of reference. This Augustinian threefold scheme heralds a conception that was not to be fully developed until modern theories of communication developed their system of the immanent correlation of various moments of information.

    Among the symbols, Augustine gives to the *word* a dominant rank and function. The word was for him the most noble symbol because in it the thing signified manifests itself of itself. Whoever forms words manifests himself as an intelligent "entity" *(res),* as a reality that predates all its symbols and which alone gives them their right sense (cf *De magistro* 10, 33; *PL* 32, 1214: "Magis signam re cognita, quam signo dato ipsa res discitur"). This peculiar character gives the word a factuality, a revelatory function, a proximity to the senses that constitutes its nobility over and above all natural symbols. The word is already the pinnacle of the whole universe of symbols because it is for the most part of intellectual-spiritual nature and so belongs to the higher sphere of being.

    (b) In this, the *ontological level* of the Augustinian theory has already been achieved. Completely in keeping with neo-Platonist idealism, he taught that every object is composed of two parts which are very different from each other: a purely spiritual, timeless, unchanging part, and a material, temporal, transitory part. This double aspect of being had for Augustine existential and ethical consequences, for it is coupled with a schema of double imperatives: enjoying and using. This is without doubt the heritage of the classical teaching concerning the "goods" (we would say today the "values"), according to which only the spiritual, timeless goods can be the objects of enjoyment; the material and temporal are merely there to be used. Therefore every individual is called, not only to make a clear differentiation between these two aspects, but to see beyond, to transcend the material goods (the symbols as well) into the realm of spiritual goods.

The earthly, material objects lend their help in this transcending to the degree that they fulfill a truly symbolic and indicative function. Nothing more is expected of them. Their designated purpose is alone to give a sensual stimulus for the step by step climb to the true objects of knowledge. The material universe receives its justification to exist alone in the fact that it contains the fingerprints of the completely other, eternal, and divine universe within it, and so is a constant reminder of it. (How distant this aspect of the Augustinian thinking on symbols can be from modern sentiments is shown, e.g., by Franz Schupp who, in imitation of Teilhard de Chardin, speaks in connection with the sacraments of a "self-finality of matter" and of material work.)[13]

(c) From the level of a philosophical ethic of goods, Augustine appears to ascend without difficulty to the *theological level.* Here he takes up the idea of man's original sin: Adam sinned to the degree that he sensually gave himself over to the transitory "symbols" instead of to the unchanging "objects." In this he fell from the given order and became a slave of mere "symbols." He perverted the movement from the material goods to the spiritual goods; he pursued the movement of transcendence in the wrong direction.

Such perversion can only be corrected by the conversion that has been made possible by the events of salvation history, most particularly by the incarnation of the Logos, the eternal Word of God. These symbols have in reality to do

with "divine things" and are therefore rightly called
sacramenta. The events occured as "holy signs," and the
salvation of man, i.e., his return to the God-given order, was
in this way made possible.

Considering his epistemological and ontological
approach, it was not difficult for Augustine to see in Christ
the Word-Symbol of God, that "inner light of truth" which
was able to illumine all, "the Wisdom of the unchanging
God" which was able to instruct all (*De magistro* 14, 45; *PL*
32, 1219). Thus it appears that he was able to establish a
connection with the Pauline and Johannine Christologies
without sacrificing one iota of his neo-Platonist system.

(d) On the level of his own *theology of sacraments,* the
aspect of salvation history, which Tertullian had already
incorporated in his own thinking, manifested itself as the
underlying basis. Most of the texts in which the word
sacramentum appears refer to the biblically attested events
which he interprets as aspects of the unchanging plan of
salvation and the eternal love of God.[14] The goal of these
events has already become a part of the life of the faithful
through baptism and the Eucharist. (Factually Augustine
knows only these two ritual sacraments.)

Baptism and the Eucharist are sacred signs for the
divine "reality" of grace and as symbols contain within
themselves a double structure: they consist in a material
element and an elucidating word. In their nature as word,
they receive a particular nobility: they are exalted, simple,
understandable, and, in all purity, effective signs of grace
and faith (*De doctr. christ.* 9, 13; *PL* 34, 70: "factu facillima et
intellectu angustissima et observatione castissima"). Their
understandability comes from a largely "natural analogy"
which exists between them and the thing signified: the water
of baptism and the inner cleansing it symbolizes; the many
grains of wheat in the eucharistic bread and the many
members in the unity of the body of Christ which they
symbolize.

Is this only a signing function? Is their effectiveness
exhausted in this "natural analogy," in an allegory of

spiritual truths? Are both of these sacraments simply interpretive symbols? It would be possible to assume this from Augustine's philosophical approach. And yet the answer turns out differently: the sacrament of Christian ritual effects what it symbolizes. It communicates that to the recipient which the analogy points up: baptism communicates cleansing, justifying faith; the Eucharist communicates the unifying power of the true body and blood of Christ (cf *Ep* 98, 9; *PL* 33, 363f). This Church Father, in spite of his Platonic-idealistic way of thinking, teaches a sacramental realism.

This uncovers an unusual difficulty in his theology. The conclusions in the speculations of his theology of sacraments are not always implicit in his philosophical premises. They are based rather upon the Scriptures and Church tradition, which Augustine wishes at all costs to loyally follow. In fact, he refers in most instances specifically to these authorities when he presents the effectual grace, at work in baptism and the Eucharist, as an objective communication of grace which transcends all epistemological processes. Another support in his realistic assertions is to be found in his Christ-centered thinking; if the sacraments are really effectual, it is because they are ultimately acts of the glorified Christ.

Students and disciples of a genial thinker are not always able to fruitfully perpetuate his teaching with its inner moments of stress. They tend rather to reduce these inherited problems to clear alternatives[15]—the balance of a "both-and" becomes a one-sided "either-or." This is exactly what happened with the Augustinian theologians of the Middle Ages. (And what important theologian of that period was not a student of Augustine?) One group (Isidore of Seville, Paschasius of Corbie) represented—primarily in their eucharistic positions—an often massive realism; another group (Rathramnus, Scotus Eriugena, Berengar of Tours) taught various forms of symbolism and spiritualism.[16] How strongly the teaching office of the Church stood, at the turn of the millennium, on the side of the "realists," is

demonstrated by the eucharistic profession of faith that
Rome required Berengar of Tours to sign in 1059. According
to this document it is heretical to think that

> the bread and wine...after the consecration is only
> sacrament and not the true body and blood of our Lord
> Jesus Christ, and that these could not be taken in the
> hands of the priest and broken, or chewed by the teeth of
> the faithful (*DS* 690).

With the Reformers of the sixteenth century, this conflict
would again flare up and provoke the decisions of the
Council of Trent. Before this, however, a new and important
turning point in the sacramental teaching of Western
Christianity occurred.

1.3.3. Thomas Aquinas

This turning point was prepared already in the twelfth
century by theologians of the University of Paris. Hugo of
St. Victor (†1141) attempted to define the sacraments—
among which he counted as well such rites as the use of holy
water, blessed ashes, the consecration of monks, and
burial—from their historical and juridical institution as
"receptacles of grace." The goal of sacramental rites,
according to him, was a kind of ecclesial pedagogy; the
faithful, through the reception of grace which was bound to
the material, were to be encouraged in their humility and
supported in their moral growth (*De sacramentis* I, 9; *PL* 176,
315-329; cf I, 12; *PL* 176, 415f). Peter Lombardus (†1160),
another Parisian teacher, continued this predominantly
ritual, moral and juridical tradition, adding new speculations as to sacramental causality. His definition was: "One
speaks of sacraments in their proper sense when a symbol of
God's grace, which is a form of invisible grace bearing its
likeness and being its source, is present."[17] This definition of
terms was to maintain its dominance in Catholic theology

up to the Council of Trent—indeed even to some degree in the neo-Scholastic theology of the present. In connection with Hugo's concept of their institution, his theories contributed in the middle of the twelfth century to their number being fixed at seven.[18]

A thorough reshaping of the Augustinian heritage, which was the basis of all these approaches, did not come until Aristotelian philosophy was applied to the theology of sacraments. This began with Hugo of St. Cher (†1263) and reached its culmination with Thomas Aquinas (†1274). Thomas shaped a synthesis, no longer with the aid of Platonic idealism, but with the *Aristotelian* emphasis on the empirical and effective.[19] In this, realism celebrated its greatest triumph over symbolism. No longer does the merely epistemological-catechetical function of ritual acts stand in the foreground, but their physical and metaphysical effect on the communicant. At the same time, the decline of the conception of supra-cultic mysteries of salvation history and of sacraments began. Their role as basis and support of all ritual acts now became less dominant than it was with Tertullian and Augustine.

For Thomas the guiding principle remained valid: the sacraments effect what they signify. That they are means of grace he explained through the efficacy of God as "principal cause" and the sacraments as "instrumental cause," which God has entrusted to his Church through Christ. In this way the seven sacramental acts can be seen as sovereign interventions of God the Creator and Savior into the human sphere. God uses ritual as an instrument for the communication of his grace, but he remains completely free in so doing. He does not bind his grace always and everywhere on the sacraments (*STh* III 72, 6 ad 1: "virtus divina non est alligata sacramentis"); he is able to effect salvation apart from sacraments. Still the normal, "regular" way of this effecting is the seven sacraments instituted by Christ. These have a structure that Thomas then describes in Aristotelian terminology. They consist of "material" and "form." Similar to the physical substances, "material" composes, according to Aristotle, the component which is capable of being shaped in a number of ways; "form," on the other hand, is the determining, shaping component. Sacramental "material" is either the visible element, such as the water of baptism or the bread and wine of the Eucharist, or the sensuous, symbolic action, such as the confession of guilt by a repentant sinner in penance. The sacramental "form" consists of the words (*STh* III 60, 8, 2), which the one administering the sacrament speaks to elucidate the element or action, e.g., the priest's words of absolution or consecration.

When the sacraments are administered in the sense of their institution by Christ and according to the will of the Church—when, in other words, the "right material" is combined with the "right form"—the sacraments infallibly effect grace. They are effected "ex opere operato" (*Sent. dist.* I, q 1, a 5; cf *STh* III 62, 4), e.g., by the very fact of the accomplished action itself, apart from the religious or moral disposition of the one administering or the one receiving the sacrament. For the effectiveness of the sacrament it is sufficient that the one administering have the intention of doing what the Church wishes to do, and that the one receiving is not closed or indifferent to God's offer of grace. The sacrament "is not accomplished through the righteousness of the one who gives or receives it," but rather "through the power of God" (*STh* III 68, 8; cf 64, 8-10).

It is evident that Thomas emphasizes the *effective causality* of God which comes to expression in the correctly developed function of the instrumental causality of the sacrament. Interest is therefore brought to bear more on the structure, function, and effectivity of the objectively conducted ritual than on that which is expected of the subject, e.g., on the "commitment of faith" or the "dialogical relationship" to the sacrament. Tertullian's decidedly ethical understanding of the sacraments, which tended to further a personal participation, is conveyed less strongly in this view.

A survey of the developing history of the theology of

sacraments in the Middle Ages (which in this introduction cannot be considered more closely) would show that the Thomistic theory was not without its critics. As a prime example of this could be mentioned the Franciscan school and, above all, Duns Scotus. For them, grace cannot be "contained" in a sacrament as an effect with its cause, as in the Aristotelian approach. "The sacramental symbols prepare for the reception of grace which God, by reason of a separate decree, confers directly" (I. Finkenzeller, art. "Sakrament," in *LThK* 9, 224). The communication of grace is then "occasioned by" the sacrament rather than through its instrumental effect.

This thinking is certainly nearer the original approach of Augustine and detracts from the cultural role of sacraments in religious experience. At the same time, other means of grace, such as personal prayer and the proclamation of God's word, take on a more central role in the Christian life.

1.3.4. The Reformers

The biblical and the Augustinian conviction that the *word* of God is the highest criterion for the constitution of Christian life and the Church is the basis for the critique of Luther, Zwingli, and Calvin against a particular sacramental realism. It is the unearned word of grace, embodied in Christ, and as such it must condemn the inflationary multiplication of eucharistic sacrifices, acts of penance, and blessings prevalent in late medieval Christianity. As the written, biblically attested *word* of revelation, it must exclude all purely "human inventions" of tradition, including all "so-called" sacraments for which no specific and clear word of institution, commission, or promise of Jesus is to be found.[20] As the determinative word of salvation, it must be able to awaken justifying grace in sinners, independent of sacramental means of salvation. Therefore Luther declares, "It is not the sacrament, but the faith of the sacrament that justifies" (*WA* 57, 169, 23). Whoever does not have faith places in vain his trust in sacraments; he receives no grace. Only one who receives the word of God directly in living, personal faith, and obeys it, can be sure of being pardoned—with or without intervening sacraments.

This has rightly been referred to as a form of "personalistic salvation." It was in fact the intention of the Reformers to establish for the individual a direct relationship to the living God. Nothing, even an ecclesiastical intervention in extreme cases, could hinder the person in finding an immediate access to the God who calls.

Which role the sacraments instituted by Jesus, i.e., baptism and the Lord's Supper (for Luther, reconciliation as well), were to play in this context, the Reformers were never able to agree upon. Among them, the various shades of the Augustinian heritage ranging from realism to symbolism were again to be found.

Luther and Melancthon represented a realistic, if not objective, standpoint. For them the sacrament had an *effective* character: "God's effective word takes the element into its service and so really brings the individual that which is expressed by the sacramentally constituting word of promise" (E. Kinder, art. "Sakramente," in *RGG* V, 1324). The human subject is called to be open and receptive; he is able to do nothing of himself. God alone works in his word, whether in sermon or sacrament. He alone effects faith and gives assurance of salvation. The power and reality of the sacramental offer of salvation go so far that, for example, even the infant becomes a "believer" through baptism, and even the unbeliever is confronted with the gift of the body and blood of Christ in the Lord's Supper (*op. cit.,* 1325).

Zwingli, on the other hand, who rejected the word *sacramentum* as unbiblical, represented a clearly *symbolic* teaching concerning baptism and the Lord's Supper. The ritual acts, according to him, function only to symbolize the purely spiritual reception of salvation, to memorialize the redeeming acts of Christ, and to serve the faithful as signs of faith and understanding. They have nothing to do with the awakening and strengthening of faith; rather they presume a faith in the communicant and in his faith community that has previously been awakened through catechesis.[21]

Calvin held a position between those of Luther and Zwingli. He rejected Zwingli's thesis that the subject of the actions in baptism and the Lord's Supper is the believer and his faith community. For him, God alone is the subject of the sacraments. He employs them to "seal" his promises and to strengthen faith. And *because* he instituted them for this purpose, they can also be human acts of profession of faith (*Institutio Christianae Religionis* IV, 14, 1). On the other hand, he departs from Luther to the degree that he subordinates radically the sacraments as means of salvation to the proclamation of the word; the sacraments serve only as attestation of the guaranteed decree of mercy, which the word has already proclaimed (*op. cit.* IV, 14, 6f). Calvin's real contribution is his revaluation of the role of the Holy Spirit as "mediator" between the heavenly Christ and the earthly elements which are received by the believing individual.[22] Without the work of God's Spirit, the presence of Christ is not possible. Without faith, which is a gift of the Spirit, the sacraments remain for the communicant empty symbols.

The teaching office of the Catholic Church saw itself challenged by the Reformers, both in the positive and the negative sense of the word. As the Council of Trent formulated for the first time a comprehensive dogmatic doctrine of the sacraments, its intention was not only to condemn the errors of the Reformers, but to overcome the practical and theoretical abuses in its own ranks. Since this Tridentine doctrine of sacraments is binding in a number of areas for the contemporary Catholic faith community, the following systematic chapter will focus on this thematic.

Chapter Two

FUNDAMENTAL QUESTIONS
OF CATHOLIC SACRAMENTAL
TEACHING

Many questions have proved to be fundamental in the historical development of Catholic sacramental teaching, at least regarding its systematizing. In some instances, they have been the object of dogmatic definition. The relevancy of such a systematizing, that would identify *general* and valid structural elements for all sacraments, was contested by Martin Luther. The meaningfulness of a doctrine of sacraments "in general" *(in genere)* is also in many respects questioned by modern-day Catholic theologians. Karl Rahner declares:

> It is the poverty of our traditional theology of sacraments that, even though there are seven different sacraments, they are all reduced to the same level, regarding both proof of their existence and treatment of their nature (*KuS,* p. 46).

Here the certainly legitimate concern for the peculiarity of each individual sacrament in its historical growth becomes evident. Still, it is not to be denied that, in addition to special features of each, there are *also* general characteristics which are identifiable in all of the various ritual acts.

The following paragraphs will therefore examine the six

"fundamental questions" which have developed during and since the Council of Trent. This reflection will include the contemporary theological discussion of sacramental effectiveness, institution, number, necessity, administration, and reception.

2.1. Effectiveness

The victory of sacramental realism in the Aristotelian synthesis of Thomas, and its Tridentine defense against diverse questions raised by the Reformers (Zwingli), explains purely historically why the question of the efficacy and effect of the sacramental symbols has received such predominant attention. This complex includes two questions: How does a sacrament work? What does it effect?

2.1.1. How Does a Sacrament Work?

> If anyone shall say that by the sacraments of the new law grace is not conferred by virtue of the performed ritual *(ex opere operato),* but that faith alone in the divine promise is sufficient to obtain grace, *anathema sit (NR* 513; *DS* 1608).

This statement of the Council of Trent is directed against the tendency to want to make the effectiveness of a sacrament—or its lack thereof—dependent upon the subjective faith of the recipient. In fact, a one-sided over-emphasis on Luther's position would not exclude this kind of reasoning. On the other hand, it must be admitted that the Reformers had grounds to suspect the expression "by virtue of the performed ritual." It could be misunderstood in the sense of a magical formula.

For this reason, Catholic Scholasticism looked for a biblical argument for the "ex opere operato" doctrine. This they found in those New Testament passages where the efficacy of baptism was explained with the help of the prepositions "of" *(ek, ex)* and "through" *(dia, per)*, or of the instrumental dative or the ablative cases; John 3:5 speaks of being born "of *(ek)* water and spirit," and Titus 3:5 of salvation "through *(dia)* the baptism of new birth," and Ephesians 5:26 of purification "in the bath of water by the power of the word." Since all of these passages point to God, Christ, or the Spirit as the actual subject who is acting and granting salvation, they are in fact capable of preventing a shortened understanding of the sacramental expression implicit in the critique of the Reformers.

A juridical narrowness was however not always avoided in the sacramental teaching which worked with the "ex opere operato" principle. An example is the statement of Pope Benedict XIV in 1747, concerning the baptism of Jewish children. He does speak against the *permissibility* of the practice of baptizing Jewish infants against the will of their parents; but still he holds that baptism administered under these circumstances is *valid* and that the children in question must be taken away from their parents and given over for rearing to believing Christians *(DS* 2562). It can be seen here that the divergence between theory and practice was great, ranging from the scriptural accent on the sovereign action of God to a highly questionable sacramental automatism.

For a more precise determination of the effectuality of the sacraments, the theologians of the high Middle Ages proposed two main theses. The Thomistic school spoke of a "physical" effectiveness in which a sacrament contains and transmits grace dynamically, as a canal does water. The basic idea behind this was, as for Thomas himself, "instrumental causality" *(STh* III 62, 5; cf *De Veritate* q 27 a 4). The progression of grace could be traced by a linear schema: God ⟶ Sacrament ⟶ Individual.

The other thesis, represented primarily by Duns Scotus and the Franciscan school, speaks of a "moral causality." Because of its divine institution and promise, the sacrament is able, in its celebration, to move God, so that he gives his gracious support to the recipient.[1] This grace, however, comes directly from God and not from a primary mediation of the sacrament. The sacrament works rather on God who in this way is reminded of his promise. Here we could present the schema: Sacrament ⟶ God ⟶ Individual.

One of the last great Scholastics of the modern period, L. Billot (†1931), proposed a further thesis, that of "intentional causality." According to this theory, the sacrament effects in the individual not so much grace itself as the disposition to the reception of grace. There arises in the recipient then a kind of "claim" to grace, which, as long as no hindrance is present, leads to its goal. According to this concept, the causal movement could be shown in the schema: Sacrament ⟶ Individual ⟶ Grace.

The typical Scholastic technicality of these attempts at explanation is unable to enthuse modern man. Major theological thinkers of the last decades were aware of this as they presented their new approaches. Three of the most important such new approaches will now be considered.

(a) *Odo Casel* (1948), Benedictine and liturgist from the Abbey Maria Laach, intended no reflection on abstract ontological questions; he approached the sacraments in their concrete ritual performance. In doing so, he widened the perspective from a more narrow consideration of the material and form of the individual sacraments to a broad interest in their complete liturgical "celebration." Only in the experiencing of the ritual is it possible for the faithful Christian to grasp their existential meaning and consciously open himself to their saving power.

Casel concentrated his interest primarily on the Eucharist, which he considered the center and the most profound concretization of the Church's sacramental economy. For his interpretation he took recourse to the Greek Church Fathers of the first five centuries who saw in the Eucharist as well as in baptism "mystery celebrations" that are best explained in the language of the ancient mystery cults and with the help of Platonic terminology. On this foundation, Casel constructed an approach that saw the sacraments as a mystery celebration in three stages. The first stage consisted in the "Easter mystery," Christ himself, i.e., in his death and resurrection. This mystery of Christ's singular "saving deeds" is made present by the second, mediating stage, the "ritual mystery." The dramatic events of the cross and the empty grave are graphically and symbolically—and therefore all the more realistically— repeated, renewed, actualized. This making present of the Easter mystery in the ritual mystery effects the third stage, the mystery of the "participation" in, of the "conforming" of the participating faithful to, the "saving deeds" of Christ and so consequently to Christ himself. "The mystery," Casel writes,

> is a sacred, ritual act in which one of the acts of salvation becomes present in the midst of the ritual; in that the cultic community celebrates this ritual, it participates in the act of salvation and thereby attains salvation.[2]

Casel certainly intended in his theology of sacraments, which gives the Platonic original/replica-concept an important role, to take into consideration the spirituality of his day, which tended toward symbolic and graphic concreteness. Joining with such Church Fathers as Cyril of Jerusalem (cf *Myst. cat.* 2, 6 and 3, 1; *PG* 33, 1081f, 1088f) he writes:

> Through the comprehension of faith we see in the sacramental replica the original itself, i.e., the saving work of Christ. We view it in faith and in gnosis; that is, we touch it, appropriate it, become conformed to it through participation, and therefore transformed into the image of the Crucified and Resurrected.[3]

(b) In his attempts at a new explanation of the efficacy of the sacraments, *Karl Rahner* takes a completely different approach. He finds his inspiration in Augustine as interpreted by Thomas, and at the same time he seeks to do justice to the legitimate concerns of Martin Luther and to the biblical economy of salvation. His main concepts are not so much "cult" and "mystery" as "word" and "grace." He contemplates not so much the cultic concretization as the existential relevance of the sacraments' ontological structure.

Rahner's theory begins with the word of God, which he understands as "promise," as an "eschatological offer" of salvation (*KuS* 25f). God made a definitive and absolute pledge of his grace as being essentially in Christ. Christ is "the sacramentally primal word of God in the history of the one human race" (*KuS* 17). Insofar as the sacraments of the Church draw on this "primal sacramentality" of Christ, their entire efficacy and validity come from him, and they contain at the same time within themselves the creative and eschatological efficacy of the word of God. This incarnate word of God, which is Christ, allows the sacramental pledge of grace to be more than "just an offer"; it becomes a word of grace which, when accepted, effectuates grace (*KuS* 16). It is effectuated "in that it is spoken in the symbol" (*KuS* 17). And this efficacy is oriented toward permanency—the sacramentally spoken word of God and Word of Christ "will not be withdrawn." It "remains spoken"; it remains permanently bound to the symbol and continues to challenge its hearers (*KuS* 26), so that they are enabled themselves to give an answer of faith. It is significant that Rahner attempts to explain the Tridentine principle of "ex opere operato" with this theory of the eschatologically pledged word of salvation—the sacraments are effective "by the very fact of the accomplished action" only because of God's irrevocable promise and the creative pledge of salvation which has become tangible in Christ.

On the other hand, an authentic concern of the Reformation is brought into consideration when Rahner declares that the sacramental word can "be spoken only in the context of faith proclamation" (*KuS* 92). It is true that the eucharistic proclamation of the death of Christ is "the most central word" of ecclesial celebration (*KuS* 76). Still this central point becomes meaningful only as it becomes an aid to a whole complex of proclamation through word and deed which lies outside the formally sacramental (cf *KuS* 93).

(c) *Edward Schillebeeckx,* for his part, sees the efficacy of the sacraments as established by the fact that they are moments of personal "encounter" between God, i.e., Christ, and the individual believer. Insofar as the term "encounter" relates to faith, it would appear that Schillebeeckx as well takes the concerns of the Reformers into consideration (cf the key term "personalistic salvation"). However this may be, his total approach remains based on Thomism, which he attempts to rejuvenate with concepts of a modern existential-philosophical anthropology. In this context, the final subject of sacramental action (Thomas spoke of "principal cause"), namely God, is seen largely in the light of human behavioral patterns. Just as an individual "reveals" his own "mystery" in moments of communication with other individuals, and thereby gives existence to his innermost being, so in like manner does God use physical forms of encounter in order to communicate his saving being to the individual. So it is primarily Christ, always visible as the man Jesus, who is the *"personal* earthly appearance of divine saving grace" (*ChSG* 25). In him appears the personal existence of God who, as historical reality and in human bodily form, is desirous of personal encounter. This is the basis of Schillebeeckx's following Christological statement:

> In the idea of the "encounter with God"...is contained an allusion to our natural existential experience. Without this worldly, human meaning of encounter, the theological concept of "encounter with God" would have no substance for us (*ChSG* 10).

With respect to the sacraments, they have a similar communicative effect. Since they are completely rooted in the reality of the Christ, who is now in heaven, and since the "heavenly Christ" "sacramentalizes" in them his "eternally present" saving work (*ChSG* 55; cf 65), they are the permanent point and means of the encounter between God and man. Christ assures the reception of grace through the sacraments (ex opere operato) as always *possible*. For they are ultimately nothing other than his deeds in institutionally ecclesial appearance (*ChSG* 63).

At this point, Schillebeeckx, the disciple of Thomas, breaks with the Aristotelian causal conception of his master and introduces the concept of a self-manifesting love:

> In the human encounter, the visible expression of love occurs in courtship and self-giving, not in the creation of a physical reality. Love is freely given and must be freely received. Therefore, the expressive gesture of love is a courting and inviting—an offering. This gesture of love has a certain *efficacy....* A strong handclasp in itself calls forth a similar response (*ChSG* 63).

The sacraments are like gestures of divine friendship toward man. As such they are a total call for a loving reponse. This is what they wish to effect when they appeal in the Church for a willingness on the part of the recipient to faith, trust, and love. Certainly here as well, the principle, which Rahner has already stated, is valid—that the offer of God effects its reception by the human partner. Still, the progression of thought here goes beyond this basic statement and demonstrates as well the part which the human individual plays in his very own and original nature as a communicative being. If the recipient of the divine offer were to be molded by the efficacy of the sacrament in a purely passive way, no real encounter would occur. Schillebeeckx speaks of a certain reciprocity, of an "interaction," even when it is not defined more closely.

> For the interior devotion with which the recipient approaches the sacrament, or rather takes part in its prayer and celebration, is more than a pre-sacramental attitude of mind; it is an entry into the heart of the Church's mystery of worship (*ChSG* 135).

Without this comprehensively personal and historically

existential activity of the faithful, the ritual would be an "untruthful sign" (*ChSG* 135).

The question "How does a sacrament work?" has thus been answered differently by Casel, Rahner, and Schillebeeckx. Their approaches were considered as examples of the really quite "pluralistic" breakthrough of the new theology of sacraments that has been so strongly influenced by the texts of Vatican II (cf Chapter 3). The accomplishments and the limitations of their investigations cannot be considered more closely here. But one critical question can hardly be avoided: Are the above mentioned theologians not proceeding from an all too idealistic conception of liturgy, proclamation, and communicative practice in the Church as to be able to really examine the "how" of sacramental experience? Are they not positing what should be, instead of what is? These questions will be considered in the last chapter.

2.1.2. What Does a Sacrament Effect?

Conscious that the sacraments are determinative for the human individual in his personally changing history, which alternates between goal-directed progress and laming estrangement, the Catholic tradition has always sought to define the existential effect of sacramental celebration. Two fundamental teachings have crystallized out of this complex: the doctrine of "sacramental grace" and that of the "sacramental character."

2.1.2.1. Sacramental Grace

In the New Testament are to be found a whole series of symbolic expressions which characterize the effect of baptism and the Lord's Supper. Baptism places the baptized into dynamic relationship with the "name," i.e., with the inner being of Jesus Christ (Acts 2:38; 8:16; 19:5; cf 1 Cor

13-16; Mt 28:19); it makes possible participation in the death (Rom 6:3) and burial of Jesus (Rom 6:4; Col 2:12); it communicates the forgiveness of sins and the gift of the Holy Spirit (Acts 2:38) as well as "cleansing" *(apelousasthe)*, and "sanctification" *(egiasthete)* (cf 1 Cor 6:11); it incorporates into the ecclesial body of Christ (1 Cor 12:13), leads to "new birth" (Jn 3:7; cf Tit 3:5), and makes possible our entrance into "God's kingdom" (Jn 3:5)—just to mention a few. The Lord's Supper unites the many communicants into the "one body" (1 Cor 10:17), makes them participants in the body and blood of Christ (1 Cor 10:16), frees from spiritual hunger and thirst (Jn 6:35), makes possible the continuing unity of Jesus and his members (Jn 6:56), gives "life" (Jn 6:35, 53), and makes resurrection and "life eternal" possible (Jn 6:54). Other rites are referred to as well, such as the "freeing" word spoken to the sinner, or the laying on of the hands of the presbyters; it says of these acts that they mediate the forgiveness of sins (Jn 20:23), e.g., a particular "gift (*charisma*, charism) of God" (2 Tim 1:6).

It may seem like an impoverishment of this rich biblical symbolism when the Council of Trent generally reduced the effect of the sacraments to a conferring of "justification" (*NR* 505; cf 509, 511; *DS* 1600; cf 1604, 1606), that is of "grace" (*NR* 509-513; *DS* 1604-1608). It may seem even more narrow and abstract to us when Scholastic theology states that the sacraments confer on the recipient "sanctifying grace" (Ott, 399). In reality, the Council is well aware of the diversity of "graces" peculiar to each sacrament—and this not just in its statements concerning baptism, Eucharist, penance, anointing of the sick, holy orders, and matrimony. It is suggested in the decree on the sacraments in general that there is a dissimilarity. According to the particular goal of each "means of grace" there is also a differentiation of the "sacramental graces" conferred, as Thomas had already taught (*STh* III 62, 2). That, in addition, the Council of Trent did not totally overlook the thought of the existential effect of grace in concrete history is shown by its statement— which may seem to us too "quantitative" in nature—that it is the sacraments "through which all true justification begins, grows, or, after its loss, is restored again" (*NR* 505; *DS* 1600). It was this guiding principle which Schillebeeckx, with a view to an existential anthropology, further developed by stating that grace can be "sacramental" only insofar as it "reveals itself by becoming history in our lives" (*ChSG* 13). Because being human always means becoming human, because this human development from childhood to death, from secular occupation to God-given vocation, is a constantly changing situation including multiple moments of danger and alienation, and because the human person must be continually personalized in the context of the supporting community, sacramental encounters with God can only consist for the individual as a permanent and flexible accompaniment (*ChSG* 25, 28, 31f, 116).

Rahner's contribution to a renewal of our understanding of grace can also be summarized. Basically, "grace" is not a thing in itself which can be objectified, including its sacramental form of appearance. It consists primarily in a self-communication of God; the giver and the gift coincide. It becomes understandable, then, that no ritual act can dispose over grace as if grace could be specified and communicated alone through the ritual. Rather it is grace which verbalizes, incarnates, symbolizes itself, communicates itself through the sign (cf *KuS* 31). As spiritual being *par excellence,* God, e.g., grace in person, breaks out of himself, takes on communicative form and, so manifesting himself, speaks to man (cf *Kus* 33-37). He does not do this in an indifferentiated manner, but rather with a view to the "individual salvation" (*KuS* 57; cf 85) of the communicant. Therefore there is a variety of sacraments—according to Rahner, as many as there are various types of spiritual situations.

2.1.2.2. Sacramental Character

A very distinct form of this differentiation of God's working is expressed in the Catholic doctrine of the so-called "sacramental character," i.e. "sacramental attribute." This was formulated officially in 1439 at the Council of Florence:

Among the sacraments there are three—baptism, confirmation, and holy orders—which impress a character on the soul, i.e., an indestructible spiritual sign, which distinguishes them from the other sacraments. Therefore they are not repeatedly administered to the same person (*NR* 504; *DS* 1313; cf *NR* 514; *DS* 1609).

Historically seen, this statement should be reversed to say that, because the three designated rites since their emergence, i.e., since their reception as sacraments (in the case of confirmation and holy orders not before the end of the fourth century), were not considered to be repeatable, the concept of their character was introduced as a theoretical corroboration. The first stimulus for this was the so-called dispute concerning schismatic baptism around the middle of the third century. It was customary during this period in the African church and in Asia Minor to rebaptize all those who came into the Church, but had been previously baptized by heretics. This practice gave rise to an extended controversy, particularly between Cyprian of Carthage and Pope Stephen I, until finally the Bishop of Rome was able to prevail around the year 255 (cf his declaration in *DS* 110). Then in the fourth century a number of theologians developed the doctrine of the "sealing of the baptized." 2 Corinthians 1:21-22 served as their basis, a text which they interpreted, seen from a modern perspective, rather arbitrarily. Again, these theological reflections received new impetus from a controversy. This was directed, at the time of Pope Miltiades (311-314), against the Donatists, who refused to accept ordinations which had been administered by apostate officeholders. The conviction, which was later supported by Augustine, finally predominated—that because the sacraments are to such an extent the work of God, their effectiveness cannot be blocked by the unworthiness of their administrator. To illustrate this concept, several similes were used, such as the marking of sheep with the sign of their owner, the tattooing of soldiers with the "sign" or "character" of their lord, and many more (for documentation cf Auer, 71-76).

These similes, which could easily be misunderstood, received a theological depth in the Scholastic doctrine of sacramental character in the high Middle Ages—most clearly through Thomas Aquinas (*STh* III 63, 2f). Thomas interpreted this character Christologically and in the sense of its function. The baptized, the confirmed, and the ordained participate in a character that is fundamentally the character of Christ himself, the living Image and eternal Priest of God. The human bearers of this "character of Christ" are not only conformed to the priestly image of Christ (cf Heb 5:5f), thus distinguishing them from other human individuals, but they are commissioned and qualified for the ritual service of God in the midst of the Church.

Karl Rahner has attempted to make this doctrine of the sacramental character—which was strictly rejected by the Reformation and is problematical for a critical hermeneutic of the Scripture—understandable for the modern mind. He rejects a mystification of the indelible spiritual seal, and wishes to find its theological content in "the permanent claim made on the baptized by the Church through a sacramental, historical occurrence" (*KuS* 79). As such, the "character" is to be understood as a "permanent social fact" (*KuS* 80), which must be concretized in ecclesial service.

It can, however, be asked critically whether biblically theological (and not purely historical) grounds can be found for such a "claim" to an ecclesial service of God and man, which is made exclusively through the sacraments of baptism and confirmation—and not, for example, through the sacrament of matrimony. In passing, it can be mentioned that several theologians have sought to overcome this difficulty with the concept of a "quasi-character."

2.2. The Institution of Sacraments

What is understood as the institution or establishment of the sacraments has, in the course of history, been variously explained and defined. It would therefore be helpful to examine several older attempts before we try to show how contemporary theologians—also in varied directions—address the "fundamental question" of the origin of the sacraments.

2.2.1. Developments Within Tradition

A very broad movement within the older tradition began with the doctrine of grace, orienting itself primarily around the idea of sacraments as signs and means of grace. But the absolute freedom of God demands that he maintain sovereign control over the means of the distribution of grace, as over grace itself. Therefore only God himself can be the source and author of the sacraments. Another approach which was based on the New Testament *mysterion* concept, was less developed, at least in Western theology. According to this approach, the ritual *mysteria*, i.e. *sacramenta,* of the Church have meaning only when their entire existence is shown as grounded in the supra-cultic *mysterion* of God— that is, when they are seen as concretizations of the one mystery of Christ. If a ritual act has nothing to do with Christ as *the* "Mystery of God" (Col 2:2), then it does not deserve to bear the title "sacrament."

The more specific designation of the context of sacramental institution also reveals strong variation. Augustine, for example, was satisfied with a primarily mystical explanation, according to which all the sacraments derive from the act of salvation which was completed on the cross. The Church Fathers did not hesitate to give John 19:34 an allegorical interpretation: "As the Lord on the cross sank into the sleep of death, the lance pierced his side, from which flowed the sacraments and through which the Church was created" Ps 126, 7; *PL* 37, 1672). Thomas Aquinas did not abide by such Christologically symbolic considerations, but suggested a solution which worked with a judicial analogy. Just as a law possesses only that value for which the lawgiver has given authority, so analogously the

sacraments—or at least their necessary components—
contain only that validity with which God, i.e., the God-man,
has endowed them (*STh* III 64, 2). Thomas answers the
objection that many aspects of sacramental ritual, indeed
entire sacraments themselves, are not at all substantiated
by the written word of God, the Bible, so that their legitimacy
as instituted by Christ cannot be established, by referring to
the unwritten tradition of the apostles. This can be seen in
Paul's statement in 1 Corinthians 11:34. Here the apostle
declares, at the conclusion of his report of the institution of
the Eucharist by Jesus, "As for other matters, I shall give
instructions when I come." For Thomas it is completely
conceivable that the apostle is speaking here in his capacity
as "representative of God" and is in all probability obeying
an oral command of the God-man; consequently he is
capable of giving instructions regarding further sacraments
as well (*STh* III 64, 2 ad 3; cf 64, 3).

The Reformers demonstrated a more critical attitude
toward "using" such biblical statements for dogmatic
purposes. They did not allow for argumentation from
"unwritten tradition" (a really quite elastic concept) in such
determinative questions. Here as everywhere, the Scriptures
alone must decide; they demanded clearly biblical "words of
institution" or "words of promise" from Jesus. All of those
rituals which cannot be demonstrated in this way, although
they might have a centuries-long tradition in the life and
practice of the Church, must be considered "false sacraments" and rejected. On the basis of this critique, the
Reformers were obliged to reject confirmation, matrimony
and the anointing of the sick as sacraments of Christ.
Nevertheless, Luther tended to maintain the sacramentality
of penance, and Calvin did not reject the possibility that
ordination to ecclesial service could be sacramental.

It can be assumed that the caution with which the
Council of Trent formulated its position concerning the
institution of sacraments shows in some respects a certain
openness to the critique of the Reformation, while at the
same time Trent's positions were meant to be clearly anti-
reformist. They state:

> Whoever says that the sacraments of the new covenant
> were not all instituted by Christ, our Lord, or that there are
> more or less than seven...he is excluded (*NR* 506; *DS* 1601).

Does the use of the name "Christ" here indicate an intended
Christological perspective modeled on Augustine, and
consequently a disassociation from any attempt to trace all
the sacraments back to the historical Jesus? It appears that
the Council did not want to go that far. In any case, it is clear
that the Tridentine decree on the sacraments says nothing
more specific about the question of their institution. It did
not opt for the theses, which long predominated in the
Middle Ages, that all seven sacraments were instituted
directly by Jesus. On the other hand, there is the counter-
position of the mediated institution of the sacraments—i.e.,
through the apostles at Jesus' command—which was
represented by such theologians as Hugh of St. Victor, Peter
Lombard and Bonaventure. In the discussion of the question
whether Christ determined the "material" and "form" of the
sacramental acts "specifically," i.e., in every particular, or
only "generically," i.e., limited to its essential goal, was
likewise ignored by the decree.

2.2.2. Currently Attempted Solutions

Current investigations no longer approach the question,
as was earlier the case, from the ritual or canonistic nature of
the sacraments. Since the reception of the historical-critical
method by theology, it has become an accepted fact that
even the words of institution for baptism and the Eucharist
cannot without hesitation be considered the "original
words" *(ipsissima verba)* of the historic Jesus. For the five
remaining sacraments, specific acts of institution by Jesus,
in the juridical sense of the term, are still less to be assumed.

In this critical context of thought, the position of the so-
called modernists around the turn of the last century is
understandable, a position which held that the sacraments

actually originated with the apostles and their successors. They interpreted certain ideas and intentions of Jesus creatively, under the influence of the ecclesial situation and in response to general human needs, and so in this way enlarged and developed Christian ritual (cf *DS* 3439f). It is evident that the interest is here no longer in a mystical, Christological, juridical, or even—in the sense of the Reformation—biblical approach. Only the historically tangible counts here. Theologically, the modernist thesis (condemned in 1907 by Pius X) tends toward the concept of an ecclesial development of sacramentality in its apostolic and post-apostolic period of consolidation.

The most recent attempts at explanation again take up the modernists' concern for tracing the interpretations and structures, which have developed within the Church, back to the original thoughts and intentions of Jesus. This has, however, been freed of all historicizing tendencies. The attempt is made to discover the intentions of Jesus to which the individual sacraments with their objectives probably correspond. Only a few examples can be given. The fact, which can hardly be doubted historically, that Jesus willingly received the baptism of John would appear to be evidence of his intention that baptism should be the rite of initiation into the kingdom of God. The practice of Jesus, which in the Gospels is clearly demonstrated, to have fellowship around the table—with both disciples and non-disciples—under the sign of the coming kingdom, is recognized as the context in which the "Last Supper," i.e., the "farewell meal" of Jesus and later the "Lord's Supper" of the primitive Church, was celebrated as a sign of eschatological brotherhood. The numerous statements of Jesus concerning his personal prophetic relationship to the Spirit of God, as well as those concerning his intention of conferring that same Spirit, give the grounds for making baptism and confirmation understandable as originating from Jesus. The numerous healings of disease by Jesus are seen as allusions to the later sacrament of the sick.

Schillebeeckx wishes to treat such basic elements of

historical reflection by presenting his thesis of the "core" and "clothing" of the sacraments. According to him Jesus determined only the "core of each sacramental symbol" (*ChSG* 118), i.e., that which is borne by its meaning and the grace it confers. This is done either by a direct expression of his will or simply by his manner of behavior (*ChSG* 120f). The "clothing" of this "core" which Jesus has determined with respect to "material" and "form," "element" and "word," is then the work of the apostolic and post-apostolic community of faith. With their God-given freedom, but also within the God-given boundaries, they worked out the symbolic material of the sacraments, taking into consideration the practical perspectives of the Church in its diverse cultural settings. Insofar as they are contemporary forms of the sacramental cult, whose "core" Jesus has determined, and insofar as they correspond to this "core," they are to be considered legitimate components of the living Christian tradition of the Church (cf *ChSG* 127f).

A comprehensive and speculative solution to the question of sacramental institution is offered by Karl Rahner in his thesis of the Church as the "original sacrament." Basic for this thesis is the idea of a three-phase sacramentality in the salvation economy of God. Christ is seen as the "original sacramental word of ultimate grace," the Church as the "original sacrament" of this Christ, and the sacraments themselves as the "self-expression" of the Church as original sacrament (*KuS* 17–22). In keeping with this is Rahner's definition:

> When in respect to an individual, in situations decisive for his salvation, the Church accomplishes one of the actions proper to her, engaging her responsibility fully, and actualizing her essence as the primal sacrament of grace, there we have a sacrament" (*KuS* 85).

If this is so, then the entire problematic of sacramental institution is moved from the cultic level to that of ecclesiology. This means that, to be able to designate the

seven "basic acts" of the Church as sacraments of Christ
and of God, it is sufficient to show that the Church, as the
ontological "point of origin" for the sacraments (*KuS* 17), is
really founded by Jesus Christ. The "institution of a
sacrament can...simply ensue from the fact that Jesus
founded the Church with its nature as original sacrament"
(*KuS* 38).

With this theory, the difficulty of finding a "word of
institution" for the individual sacraments is in itself
resolved (cf *KuS* 40-56). The need, which is often expressed,
to date the institution of all the sacramental rites from the
apostolic Church also ceases. The fact, for example, that the
sacramentality of matrimony and of holy orders first
emerged in the fourth century cannot infringe on their
legitimacy. The important thing is that they were understood—from a particular time onward—as explicit "self-
expressions of the Church in the crucial sphere of salvation." Ultimately this opens the way to a Church which is in
principle free and is able to determine changes, developments, and modes of celebration in the area of the sacraments. Even the number of sacraments would be at the
disposal of the Church as the ontologically "permanent
presence of Christ" in the world (*KuS* 17).

The systematic inclusiveness of this thesis has not
failed to have its effect on the contemporary Catholic theology of sacraments. Still, a series of critical questions must
yet be answered. At the outset it must be asked: With what
justification is the Church—in reference to the concept of
that mystery of the one mystery of God, which is Christ
himself—referred to as "original sacrament"? Is this not a
projection of the Augustinian and, what is more, of the
Thomistic concept of sacraments onto the Church as an
idealized collective whole? Does the analogy between the "ex
opere operato" effectiveness of the signs of grace and that of
the Church play a role? And, lastly, regarding the historical
dimension, can a real and direct institution or founding of
the Church by the historical Jesus (with or without original
sacramental character) be posited? If not, exactly how is the

founding of the Church—which at the same time would imply the universal institution of all the sacraments—to be perceived? Is it at all possible to solve historical difficulties with ontological-theological argumentation?

These questions, which testify to an academic deficit in Catholic sacramental theology, should not however conceal the dogmatic constants: sacramental authority is founded alone on its relationship to Christ, and this has to be an historical relationship. Perhaps it would help to observe the nuances of the concept "foundation"; it does not refer so much to a (juridical) instituting or founding as it does to an establishment of its foundations in the context of salvation history.

2.3. The Number of Sacraments

The Council of Trent rejected the idea that there are "more or less than seven" sacraments (e.g., baptism, confirmation, Eucharist, penance, extreme unction, holy orders, and matrimony), or that "one of these seven is not actually and really sacramental" (*NR* 506; *DS* 1601).

Behind this dogmatic formulation there is an extended development. As binding teaching of the Church, something is here stated that cannot be found in any official document of the Church or in any theological system until the twelfth century. The historical survey in Chapter One shows that even Augustine was thinking primarily of baptism and the Eucharist when he spoke of sacramental rites. It is true that the Augustinian definition of sacraments provided the instrument for a clearer differentiation between those ecclesial rites that were understood as sacraments and those that were not. Still, theologians were not able to bring the process of clarification to a conclusion for another eight hundred years. The number of the sacraments varied according to the theologian.[4] In the tenth century, the Western Church began to recognize the sacramentality of penance and matrimony in addition to baptism and the

Eucharist; beyond this there were various anointings, which were components of rites of consecration, such as in baptism, confirmation and the consecration of kings, priests, and monks. The number in question varied from five to twelve; indeed some theologians counted as many as thirty. The preparation of a theory based on firm principles was largely the accomplishment of Thomas Aquinas. It was he who made the list of seven sacraments into a theologically well-corroborated doctrinal statement.

Thomas proceeds from the understanding that the sacraments are directed toward the perfecting and the spiritual healing of humanity. But people as individuals, as well as members of ecclesial and secular society, must be perfected and healed. With regard to personal human development, three elements are recognizable: conception, the growth of the body-soul, and nourishment. These three existential moments correspond in the religious realm to baptism (as spiritual rebirth), to confirmation (as strengthening in the Holy Spirit), and to the Eucharist (as the true bread of life). Because the human individual is constantly endangered in his bodily and spiritual integrity, and therefore is often sick, penance and the anointing of the sick (Thomas still calls this "extreme unction") are sensible and necessary. On the other hand, the social nature of the individual demands that he live, prosper, and be formed in community. Holy orders is directed toward this need for communal guidance, and matrimony to the need for the propagation and development of the race (*STh* III 65, 1). The individual needs no more. The seven natural functions of life encompass the entire breadth of existence—the seven sacraments do the same.

Thomas' intention to construct a hierarchical order among the seven ritual sacraments is a typical concern of the medieval period. This he did by asserting the criterion that those rites, which touch the individual in his essence as person, logically precede those of more social character. For this reason holy orders and matrimony are found at the end of his list. Those sacraments, which are designed for the restoration of the ill and injured, are to be classified after those which are continual supports to religious existence; therefore penance and the anointing of the sick come after baptism, confirmation, and the Eucharist (*STh* III 65, 2). The most perfect of all sacraments, in one decisive respect, is the Eucharist. It stands at the pinnacle of the hierarchy for two important reasons: first, because it not only contains the power of Christ, but Christ himself in his entirety; and, second, because all other sacraments are related to it and are clustered around it. In this sacrament alone is perfected the great comprehensive vital communication between Christ and his community (*STh* III 65, 3).

This speculative organization of the sevenfold economy of grace certainly does not find its power to convince in a meticulously scientific historical research, but rather in a desire to comprehend the meaning of the sacraments, which are existentially to be found in the Church, in their anthropological function. This, and not merely the fact that there are seven, is seen by modern Catholic theology as determinative.

There may very well be completely other reasons for the number seven which are to be found in cultural history. Knowledgeable researchers assume that this number was gradually accepted because of its mystical significance. The pre-Christian philosophers, the Jewish Platonist Philo, and Augustine all ascribe to the number seven the symbolic meaning of totality, universality, and inclusiveness. As the sum of three, the symbol for the divine, and four, the symbol of cosmic perfection, seven appears as a mystical, holy quantity. It was then most natural for the medieval theologian that those rites, which effected in Christian ritual the great communication between God and man, should be constructed according to this numerical pattern.

In spite of all speculative efforts to hold fast to this arduously devised structure, the multiplicity of Church traditions often resulted in its being riddled. So, for example, anointing as the sacrament of "extreme unction" was dropped in the Oriental church and became in many areas a yearly rite oriented toward the forgiveness of sins. Further, the Eastern form of penance did not correspond to the Western sacrament of reconciliation in that it was conferred by monks, i.e., non-priests (cf Auer, 92). In the West, there has been from time to time a hesitancy regarding the unity or the independence of baptism and confirmation. And it is still possible to interpret in the sacrament of holy orders various sacramental steps. Karl Rahner writes:

> It is open to any Catholic theologian to regard diaconate, priesthood and episcopate as the articulation or distribution of the one power of order derived from Christ. This is all the more so because all the great theologians of the Middle Ages conceived the lower grades of order as sacramental, and it is even now permissible to consider that they were then true sacraments, even if one wants to maintain that they are so no longer" (*KuS* 65).

According to the historical and theological spectacles through which one is looking, it is still possible, on this basis, to count as many as nine sacraments (*KuS* 65). Here, of course, the question must be asked: If there were sacraments earlier which are no longer considered as such, is it not possible to conceive that in the future there could be sacraments which at present are not understood to be such?

Apart from this kind of historical reflection and consideration of possibilities, it would appear that Thomas' anthropological approach permits relativizing. When, for example, Schillebeeckx speaks of "*the* seven prime moments of human existence" (*ChSG* 182), or K. Rahner of the seven "situations decisive for salvation" (*KuS* 85) which call forth the absolute apostolic mission of the Church as original sacrament, what is the criterion for determining what a "prime moment" or an "occasion of salvation" is, or is not? Would it not be possible in a contemporary setting to interpret the choice of profession, a business undertaking, a long and dangerous trip, emigration, a change of residence, etc., as such "moments" or "occasions," and therefore to call for a sacramental mediation of grace by the Church?

The final impression of the doctrine of seven sacraments is one of broad flexibility and relativity. Therefore it seems extremely incongruous when Schillebeeckx, referring to the question of the number seven, posits this as an ontological question and speaks of the "sevenfold grace" of God (*ChSG* 119). It would be approaching the concern of the total tradition of the Church more closely when, proceeding from that which has de facto developed (including the seven sacraments as they have been presented to us), this is simply accepted and the meaning of their sacramentality is examined. Then the question of their quantity, the theoretical problem of their number, no longer stands in the foreground, but rather the question of the actual meaning and effectiveness of the existing sacraments for our salvation. Only in this way can the intention of the sacramental economy of God's salvation, which has existed since the earliest Christian period, be approached. The ritual acts must remain existentially and practically relevant; theoretical discussion can grow only out of living practice.

2.4. The Necessity of Sacraments

The consciousness that God's economy of grace is more comprehensive than its ecclesial, sacramental mediation has been more or less present and effective in the various stages of Catholic doctrinal development. In any case, it was never completely displaced, not even by such a "sacramental enthusiast" of the Middle Ages as Thomas Aquinas. He did not hesitate to defend clearly and energetically the view, which had so often been outlined by Augustine, that "the divine power to save is not shackled to the sacraments" (*STh* III 72, 6 ad 1). This recognizes the sovereign freedom of God's self-communication and work of salvation. Or, to use New Testament terminology to express Thomas' position, the *mysterion* of the universal offer of salvation develops in history in other ways than merely through ritual acts of the Church. This was clearly indicated by Vatican II when it declared that salvation is attainable as well outside the visible fellowship of the Catholic Church.[5]

The traditional argumentation, therefore, does not necessarily boil down to the generalization that all sacraments are absolutely necessary for salvation, but rather to a varied insight into their "appropriateness." This means that the existence and use of the Church's seven signs of grace is not "absolutely necessary," but only "highly appropriate" ("necessitas convenientiae" or "congruentiae") (Ott 408). The sacraments are appropriate, to begin with, in view of the social nature of the Church, i.e., of its "visibleness." How could such a community of faith exist without clearly tangible symbols of common faith and acquired salvation? Further, the signs of grace are suited to stem that ever lurking "gnostic" arrogance which supposes itself capable of attaining religious enlightenment by purely private and spiritualized means. The sacraments are also appropriate in traditional understanding because of their effectiveness in challenging and furthering the basic attitudes of faith, trust, and love of neighbor. They awaken faith and trust in that they are "pledges" of the divine promise of salvation. They foster love in their ecclesial-communal celebration in that they strengthen the consciousness of solidarity in the concrete group where they are communally celebrated (Ott 408; cf *STh* III 61, 1; *Catech. Rom.* II 1, 9).

Although the argument concerning appropriateness was usually placed first by Catholic doctrinal tradition, still the Council of Trent felt it prudent to speak of "necessity":

> Whoever says that the sacraments of the new covenant are not necessary for salvation, but rather are superfluous, and that it is possible for men without them, or without a desire for them, to attain from God the grace of justification through faith alone—though, of course, not all are necessary for each individual—he is excluded (*NR* 509; *DS* 1604).

How is it possible to interpret this statement correctly? It is, as a whole, a negative statement which is directed against the idea that the sacraments of the Church are superfluous because justification of the sinner ultimately is possible "through faith alone." Whether Luther, who is here being referred to, in fact spoke in this sense of the three sacraments which he recognized need not be considered. In any case, the contention of the Council that the sacraments are necessary for salvation stands in opposition to a movement to exclude them from the salvation process.

Beyond this, the Council in its statement did not neglect to avoid the assertion of the absolute necessity of sacraments for salvation in that it included two relativizing clauses. In the first place, it stated that not all sacraments are for every individual believer indispensable. This particularly points up the *theology* of sacraments and, consequently, a certain order of priority among them regarding their "necessity." Baptism and reconciliation come then to the fore in that they function to rescue the individual from the sphere of depravity and bring him back, i.e., reintroduce him to the sphere of salvation. With respect to the ecclesial fellowship of the faithful, the sacrament of holy orders receives a prominent place; without these official functions, the Church, as the social sphere in which salvation is achieved, cannot exist (cf *STh* III 65, 3f). And, further, it is admitted that even the sacraments which are "necessary" for salvation are relative in that they can be supplanted by a "desire," a *votum sacramenti*. What is meant by this "desire," and how it can be experienced, for example, in the faith-life of certain candidates for baptism will be considered later.

2.5. The Administration of Sacraments

The current theology of sacraments tends to rational categories and therefore sees the "fundamental question" concerning the administration of sacraments as a question of the (primarily interactive) relationship between giving and receiving subjects. This was quite different in the case of traditional Scholasticism, whose roots in theological history are to be found in medieval and classical categories of thought. It usually considered the question of "minister" and "recipient" separately, and the first consideration was always for the administrator. J. Auer even views in this traces of a "feudal social concept" (Auer 30). Because this second chapter is devoted primarily to the genesis of doctrinal development, this traditional division will be maintained. To begin with, the question concerning the administrator will be considered in a double perspective: Who is he? What conditions should he fulfill?

2.5.1. Who Is the Administrator of Sacraments?

The strongly developed sense of calling and service which characterized those who first proclaimed the Christian message (cf 1 Cor 4:1; 2 Cor 5:20) determined as well in the post-apostolic period the self-conception of ecclesial office-holders who were entrusted with the administration of baptism and the Lord's Supper. It was therefore a part of their sacramental service to continually point to the author of every ritual mediation of grace.

Augustine reflected this consciousness when he wrote in his commentary to John 1:33, "Whenever someone is baptized with the baptism of Christ, he should believe that he is being baptized by Christ, for of him alone is said, 'It is he who is to baptize with the Holy Spirit'" (*Contr. Ep. Parm.* II 11, 23; *PL* 43, 67). And elsewhere: "Peter may baptize, but it is He (i.e., Christ) who baptizes; Paul may baptize, but it is He who baptizes; Judas may baptize, but it is He who baptizes" (*In Ioan. tr.* 6, 7; *PL* 35, 1428). The reference to the betrayer was conditioned by the contemporary situation. Augustine is surely alluding to the disciples of Donatus, the Donatists, who made the effectiveness of a sacrament dependent upon the faith and moral quality of its human administrator. A similar problematic occupied those theologians of the third century who were involved in the so-called dispute concerning "heretical baptism." The negative result this confrontation could have for a later Scholastic systematizing of the doctrine of sacramental administration must be expressly considered.

The positive results of this controversy can be seen in the realization that the "primary administrator" of all sacraments is, in his glorified existence, the eternally contemporary Christ, and not a human agent. Although this doctrine was never formulated by the teaching office with ultimate binding force, it remained a constant of Catholic (and main-line Protestant) tradition. Pius XII expressed this in connection with the thought of the mission of Jesus and the Church, and included within this scope as well non-sacramental acts of mediated grace: "It is the divine Savior...who, through the Church, baptizes, teaches, rules, looses, binds, offers, and sacrifices (*Mystici Corporis* 57). No less Christ-centered is the doctrine of Vatican II, which, referring to Augustine, emphasizes the effective and powerful presence of Christ in the proclamation, sacramental celebration, and prayer of the faith-community (cf *SC* 7/1). The Council had both the concretely celebrating community (cf Mt 18:20) and the hierarchical structure of the Church in mind. In reference to the latter it stated:

> In the bishops, therefore, for whom priests are assistants, our Lord Jesus Christ, the supreme high priest, is present in the midst of those who believe. For sitting at the right hand of God the Father, he is not absent from the gathering of his high priests, but above all through their excellent service he is preaching the Word of God to all nations and constantly administering the sacraments of faith to those who believe (*LG* 21:1).

With this, the second constant of tradition is addressed, the "secondary minister" of the sacraments; he is an individual commissioned and sent by the "primary minister." Apart from matrimony and certain instances of emergency baptism, this commissioning is identical with ordination to the episcopacy, to the priesthood, and, in part, to the diaconate. In this sense, the Council of Trent rejected a doctrinal opinion which it, with more or less justification, universally ascribed to the Reformers: "Whoever says that all Christians have authority over the word and for the administration of all the sacraments, he is excluded" (*NR* 515; *DS* 1610). Which sacraments are reserved exclusively to the ordained office-holders is, of course, not stated in this negative decree of the Council. In the face of an extremely complex history of sacramental administration in East and West, it is indeed difficult at this point to take a position with respect to all the individual details. The fact that it is not the priest, but rather the couple themselves who "interactively" administer the sacrament of matrimony to each other, has never been seriously disputed. Regarding baptism, it has been held from ancient times that, in spite of the "institutional words" of Jesus in Matthew 28:16-20, which were addressed to the "eleven disciples," i.e., to the "apostles," anyone—indeed even an unbaptized individual—can validly if illicitly baptize. The sacrament of reconciliation was, and still is, in the Oriental church usually a "monk's confession"—that is, the forgiveness of sins is mediated by (certainly cloistered) Christians who are not priests. The specific right of bishops or priests to confer the sacraments of holy orders, confirmation, and anointing of the sick has seldom been denied. Still, current discussion of the legitimacy of non-Catholic celebrations of the Lord's Supper or of an "emergency Eucharist" without a presiding priest shows how little the Tridentine doctrine of the "secondary administrator" can be the last word.

In this context belongs, in part, the manner in which Vatican II proceeds from a concrete celebration of the sacraments that emphasizes less the exclusive right of administering sacraments by ordained office-holders as the participation of all community members (cf esp *SC* 11; 21/2; 27/2; 48; 50/1). More to this later. For now, it is sufficient to emphasize that, for the last Council, sacramental celebration is as much a concern of the concrete ecclesial group, in which a reciprocal solidarity plays a determinative role as it is a matter of the supporting proclamation and existential ritual celebration.

2.5.2. What Conditions Should the Minister Fulfill?

This question became acute in the same controversial context as that of the "primary minister," where the argument concerning heretical baptisms and the Donatists led to an attempt to determine the minimum requirement for validity which a minister must meet. The answer, which the Council of Trent gave, represents, then, the rich fruit of a long tradition:

> Whoever says that the minister who finds himself in a state of mortal sin cannot bring about or confer a sacrament, even though he has observed everything essential for the accomplishment and communication of a sacrament, he is excluded (*NR* 517; *DS* 1612).

And further:

> Whoever says that baptism, although administered in the name of the Father, and of the Son, and of the Holy Spirit, and with the intention of doing what the Church does, but administered by a heretic, is no true baptism, he is excluded (*NR* 535; *DS* 1617).

Neither the state of grace nor orthodoxy is required of the minister as a condition of validity, only that he conduct the rite correctly, as specified by the Church and in keeping with the Church's intention. These are certainly minimal conditions for those borderline cases in which the subjective fitness and worthiness of the administrator are so negligible that alone God's unerring will to save and his sense of justice can guarantee the effectiveness of that which the celebrated ritual intends and should bring about. To make of such minimal conditions and of such an appeal to the powerful self-communication of God an excuse for an amoral and faithless administration of sacraments would certainly not correspond to the intention of Church tradition.

Several modern theologians find this last thought sorely lacking in the considerations of Scholasticism. They therefore attempt to place, rather than the minimal, the optimal example at the center of their reflection; and this optimal example they understand as the norm for the normal situation. Schillebeeckx writes:

> The normal situation required strictly by the fullness of the Church's being is that of a sacramental administration in which the minister performs the acts of his office in such a way that they are at the same time an expression of his own personal dedication to the apostolate, and of his will really to sanctify the persons to whom he administers the sacraments (*ChSG* 107).

The measure of a sacramental celebration, which is not just "valid" but is a genuine answer to the divine call, is to be sought in the consciousness of the leader of the celebration, who activates his personal faith and existentially applies it in an expression of sincere testimony. In this consciousness, the "objective" testimony of the Church and its basic aim should be one and the same with the subjective testimony and the actual aim of the administrator; and this is clearly possible only when the total life-style of the individual derives from the logic implicit in his ecclesial function (*KuS* 91–93). This infers not only piety, conscientiousness, and an earnest attentiveness to the interests of the sacramental recipients. This ethos of sacramental administration includes as well real and factual proficiencies (e.g., psychological and didactical), or at least the continuous desire to optimally acquire them. Otherwise it is possible that the ritual is celebrated by a pious individual and is guaranteed by the unfailing divine promise of salvation, but the addressee scarcely feels himself spoken to; a cleft develops between the intention of the sacrament and the concrete experience of the target group or individual. The ethos of sacramental administration, which reflects on the importance of practical proclamation, cannot emphasize strongly enough the investment of personal good sense, intelligence, competence and culture.

One more practical point. The view of Vatican II that a sacramental celebration is, directly or indirectly, always the concern of the total concrete community of faith can certainly be interpreted in the sense that the community as a whole is obligated as well to strive for the previously mentioned ethos; in this way, the community certainly is co-responsible for, even if not a co-administrator of, the sacramental history of salvation which it embraces.

2.6. The Recipient of Sacraments

Jesus demanded much of the recipient of his message: an unconditional acceptance of the coming kingdom of God, a change of attitude *(metanoia)*, a living faith in God and his eschatological prophets—all demands that touched the core of the individual and were motivations for a new kind of "ethical disposition." And Jesus was not at all willing to offer access to salvation and entrance to the community of faith at a reduced price. The demands of his message counted at the same time as conditions for eschatological salvation. Everything was to be determined by a sincere attitude of faith and a willingness for change on the part of the "recipient"; this was to be possible without moral perfection, a high degree of spiritual refinement, or a scrupulous fulfilling of ritual laws.

In the primitive Church, where the rites of baptism and the Lord's Supper were established forms of community life, much was again demanded for entrance into the community and participation in the salvation offered there. No baptism without faith (cf Acts 2:41; 8:12, 37; Mt 28:19; Mk 16:16). And no baptism without "repentance" which included the renunciation of a sinful life-style (cf Acts 2:38). And above all, no baptism without a previous proclamation of God's

Word—whether in a quick and shortened form (cf Acts 8:31f; 10:34-48), or in a longer form of catechesis (Acts 8:4-25). It is not by chance that, in Acts, becoming a Christian through baptism is referred to with the stereotyped expression, they "accepted the word of God" (Acts 8:14; 2:41f *passim*).

That the Lord's Supper could not be received in whatever state of mind or ethical disposition is shown especially in 1 Corinthians 11:17-34. Here several "unworthy" attitudes (cf v 27) are mentioned: divisions in the faith community, social indifference, embarrassment of "those who have nothing," a lacking self-examination of conscience. In short, those who participate in the love feast of Christ are not to allow this rite of brotherly unity to degenerate into a dishonest, hypocritical act.

Not until the third and fourth centuries did the already mentioned dispute concerning the value of sacraments celebrated in heretical circles cause the theologians of the Church to develop certain minimal demands for the recipient of sacraments. In this context, Augustine's statement is to be understood: "The purity of baptism is completely independent of the purity or impurity of the conscience of either administrator or recipient" (*Contra Litt. Petiliani* II 35, 82; *PL* 43, 287f). It is clear that this Church father did not intend this to be a rationalization for an "impure" or even faithless reception of sacraments; it was more of an indication—made necessary by a confused ecclesiastical and political situation—that God alone can guarantee the integrity of the sacramental communication of grace. Over and above this, Augustine held firmly to the demand of the first Christians for an honest act of faith on the part of the recipient. This faith did not need to be (notice the nuance!) an orthodox faith, conforming in all particulars to the Creed, but rather had to be an act of trust in the person of Christ and God which was as honest and informed as possible (cf *De bapt.* III 14, 19; *PL* 43, 146). In modern form it could be said that it is not *what* one believes but rather *that* one believes which is finally, in God's eyes as well, the deciding factor in gaining salvation.

The Scholasticism of the Middle Ages, and to some

degree post-Tridentine Scholasticism, remained bound to a quite minimalistic (and therefore less scriptural) position. In general it taught that "for the validity of sacraments, from the perspective of the recipient, neither orthodoxy nor a moral disposition is necessary" (Ott 413). This statement presupposes a difference between a "valid" and a "worthy" reception. The interest here is in a sacramental celebration which, on the one hand, establishes rights and duties for the recipient in such a way that its reception can be "still valid," but on the other hand so preserves the basic demands made by Christ and the Church that it bears fruit for the recipient.

Regarding its mere validity, Scholastic tradition holds that, among those elements which are not necessary, but which can be achieved, is the intention of the recipient to really accept what is offered him in the sacrament. The support for this teaching is the ecclesial tradition that "it is contradictory to the Christian religion to force anyone, completely contrary to his will and in spite of his objections, to accept and observe Christianity."[6] In this sense the Council of Trent too spoke of a "free and willing acceptance of grace and gifts" (*NR* 798; *DS* 1528).

The question as to what kind of intention is necessary for the valid reception of sacraments is again answered by the Scholastics with regard to borderline cases (and thereby still setting general norms).

> The habitual intention is usually sufficient on the subjective side. In cases of emergency (loss of consciousness, mental disturbance) the sacrament may be administered when it can be reasonably assumed that the recipient, before the emergency occurred, at least implicitly had the desire to receive the sacrament.... On the objective side, the intention to receive what the Church offers is sufficient (Ott 414).

These are, of course, again minimum requirements, whose determination may very well be clear from the pastoral standpoint. Nevertheless they are difficult to harmonize with the facts of the New Testament. And, in addition, they could encourage a false conception of the right relationship between divine and human freedom if they are seen as independent of the conditions for a "worthy" and "fruitful" reception which God's will intends.

What the Church teaches in this respect bears the greatest degree of certainty *(de fide)* that can be given to a doctrinal statement according to the customary standards of dogmatic theology: "For a worthy and fruitful reception of the sacraments, a moral predisposition is required for the adult communicant" (Ott 414). For adult baptism and penance this consists in faith and repentance; a lack of such faith or repentance would be tantamount to a "hindrance to faith," to an *obex,* which was emphasized by the Council of Trent (*NR* 511; *DS* 1606). Regarding the other sacraments, the so-called "state of grace" is required, i.e., the absence of serious sin and guilt; without this, God's sacramental work of salvation experiences a "hindrance" (for the Eucharist cf *NR* 587; *DS* 1161; cf 1647).

What happens then in such a case of "hindered" sacramental celebration when its reception is "valid" but "unworthy" and "unfruitful"? According to the opinion of conventional dogmatics, in the case of those sacraments which cannot be repeated, a delayed or subsequently accruing grace is possible. As soon as the "hindrance"— whether lack of faith, lack of repentence, or serious sin—is removed, the saving efficacy, which God has promised and truly conferred, takes effect. Augustine taught this in reference to baptism: "That which has already been given begins then to effect salvation when the former lack of repentance is replaced by true repentance" (*De bapt.* I 12, 18; *PL* 43, 119).

This process, to which Scholastic tradition has given the somewhat misleading designation "revitalization" *(revivi-scentia),* is, in the case of baptism, confirmation, and holy orders, attributed to the "character," that "indelible spiritual mark," which they confer. By the power of this "character," which is conferred even in view of an "unworthy" reception, the communicant receives a kind of "claim" to the efficacy of grace. In that moment when his unfitness—which he has himself more or less caused—ceases, that grace which the sacrament offers becomes fully efficacious.

It is the opinion of a number of theologians that, in addition to the three sacraments referred to, this delayed efficacy is also possible for matrimony and the anointing of the sick. For reconciliation this is not possible because the "unworthy" reception of the sacrament results in its "invalidity." And lastly, in the case of the Eucharist, because it can be received as often as one desires, a "hindered" Communion can be virtually "transcended" by a "worthy"—or, to use a Pauline term, "appropriate"—Communion.

The clarification of such questions, which usually appear in connection with that of the *minimal conditions* for the reception of sacraments, no longer stands at the center of the reflection of present day theologians. They shift the accent—similarly as with the question of the administrator—more to the question of what must occur in order to do justice, in a practical way, to the theological existence and basic intention of sacramental celebration. Here the predominant perception is that the celebration of sacraments, on the level of religious experience, has less to do with hidden causes and legal legitimacy as with an interpersonal experience of grace. This means perceiving the sacramental celebration—in the sense of modern existential philosophy—as a completely reciprocal exchange between human individuals, as a personal relationship between "those celebrating," i.e., between the minister and the recipients. Seen and practiced in this way, the reception of the sacraments should become the concrete responsibility of the faith-community. Present day emphasis on personal freedom and the individual, along with a biblically based interest in history and community, plays the decisive role in these considerations. So it is that Schillebeeckx can state that "it belongs to the essence of a sacrament that it is directed toward particular human individuals" (*ChSG* 93) as an event of encounter between God and man. The sacrament, seen in its concrete character, is no institution in itself, but rather is a subject-oriented event and therefore, simultaneously, a community-event of the Church. The addressee remains always the believing and communicating individual in the context of his own personal history.

This is, of course, true not only in the sense of a subjective but still passive experiencing and receiving. The receiving subject is, according to this concept, by no means a consumer of sacraments, "pampered" by God and the faithcommunity. He is called to an active reception; he is expected, in keeping with his own personal character and situation, to participate in the sacramental event. It can be said, then, that the interior and exterior participation of the "con-celebrant" belongs as well to the essence of the sacramental act (*ChSG* 135). When the sacraments, from the earliest days, are called *sacramenta fidei*, this is not only because they are—as Tertullian emphasized—*acts of faith* by the faithful. By every reception of a sacrament, the personal aspect must be expressed in such a way that the sacramental event is understood, not only as the act of God and the act of the Church, but as the inner act of faith by the communicant (cf. *KuS* 104).

In applying these considerations to the two "main sacraments" (*sacramenta maiora*), it can be said that the candidate for baptism is called to the already existing faith of the Church (*KuS* 78), called to profess this faith in word and deed. Insofar as this self-action at the moment of baptism is not possible for infants, and the new Christian life, which begins in this way, is supported completely by God's "prevenient grace" and the "faith of the community" (the parents, sponsors, other members of the faith-community), the necessity arises that the child be led, as soon as he has gained the ability of decision, to a conscious, personal commitment of faith. This necessity the sacramental order of the Church sees particularly addressed in the sacrament of confirmation. In this sacrament, the candidate substantiates, ratifies, "confirms" the commitment of baptism himself. He makes the "yes," which his parents and sponsors spoke for him, into a "yes" of his own, personal, free act of faith.[7] In a similar way, the Eucharist is not only a pious partaking of the body and blood of Christ, but a "renewed, personally ratified, deepened" participation (*KuS* 74) in the ecclesial "body of the Lord," a freely actualized *yes* to being incorporated into the concrete history of the faith-community.

The benefit of this emphasis on the historical dimension of life and community is great. On the one hand is the eschatological dimension of "being underway" that points up the Christian life as a "becoming Christian" in the fold of the "pilgrim people of God"—as it is understood in the New Testament; on the other hand, the anthropological dimension is underlined, which Thomas had asserted in his defense of the "seven" sacraments—i.e., every life, including a life as disciple of Jesus, is a process of growth and maturation which, therefore, is always in danger of stagnation and decadence. It is, then, by no means sufficient to ask the question concerning the punctual and isolated reception of the sacraments, in reference only to the here and now of the celebrated rite and its "potential of grace." Attention must be expanded to include the entire process of becoming, which could be called the "sacramental life history" of an individual. At this point, dogmatics leads understandably into the area of pastoral practice.

Chapter Three

MAIN EMPHASES IN THE HISTORICAL AND CONTEMPORARY DOCTRINE OF INDIVIDUAL SACRAMENTS

The confines of this book do not allow an extensive treatment of the Catholic doctrine of the seven individual sacraments. It would, however, be substantially incorrect to leave the individual *peculiarities* of each sign of grace unmentioned, especially since they precede every general systematic analysis, historically and logically. Before any doctrine of the sacraments in general existed, there was an extensive and rich literature on the individual ritual celebrations of the Church—especially on baptism and the Eucharist, which were justifiably seen as the two main pillars of the ritual-sacramental order. Both of these *sacramenta maiora* and the five rites which are considered in the Catholic Church today as "true and actual sacraments" (Trent) were again and again reflected upon and interpreted in the course of history—with varying intensity and emphasis, as will be shown. And this is still the case. Especially that far-reaching movement which, before and after Vatican II, and especially *during* this Council, pointed Catholic theology to its biblical foundations and, at the same time, to the scope of understanding presented in modern thought categories, set totally new emphases for the doctrine of sacraments than in more traditional Scholasticism. This will be treated in this chapter along with a description of the traditional doctrine which was stated by the Council of Trent, so that the reader can receive a more or less factual picture of the theoretical and practical formulations of a ritual system which seeks to do justice to a very mobile cultural environment without losing touch with its own identity and origin.

If we examine the texts of the Council, which here will be considered prime sources, it becomes clear that, qualitatively and quantitatively, a certain overemphasis in its considerations is placed on four sacramental complexes: baptism, Eucharist, holy orders, and matrimony. Confirmation is almost exclusively treated in connection with baptism. Concerning the two "therapeutic" sacraments, penance and the anointing of the sick, the Council texts have surprisingly little to say. At first glance, this gives the impression that the main emphasis which guided their understanding is unilaterally placed on the positive and constructive elements affecting the life of the faithful. In fact, this is in keeping with the strongly pastoral and practical theological goal present in the Council's considerations.

Such a goal was, of course, not first set in the context of the last universal synod. All of the already quoted reformers of Catholic sacramental teaching had made this goal their own long before the Council. Their primary intention was to open the ritual and conceptual system, which had become, in the course of the post-Tridentine context of the Counter-Reformation struggle, welded into a rigidity in which the doctrine of sacraments, more often than not, became a part of canon law; they wished to develop a theory and practice which was anthropologically enlightened, real-to-life, and did justice to the areas of human freedom and community. They employed in this—as already often mentioned—the various impulses offered by research into the Hellenistic mystery cults, renewed biblical studies, historical and existential philosophy, and the esteem of personalism and humanism for material and corporal values.

3.1. Baptism

The fact that baptism along with the Eucharist as the "sacrament of unity," and matrimony and holy orders as the socially oriented permanent sacraments, take a prominent place in the various Council texts is certainly a rediscovery of their *fundamental function* in the life of the Church. Stated differently, baptism has broken out of its former privateness and has again been recognized in its function as initiation into the faith community which is its source and, at the same time, is constituted by it.

3.1.1. The Sacrament of Initiation— The Beginning of Personal Faith-History

In the conventional Scholastic teaching on the sacraments, the accent was clearly on the primarily individual effect of the sacrament as administered. Three such effects were usually mentioned: (a) the lending or "pouring in" of justifying grace through which "original sin" is taken away and the soul is healed; (b) the remission of all punishment for sins so that the one baptized escapes the threat of hell and becomes a candidate or aspirant for heaven; (c) the imprinting of the "baptismal character" as a "seal" of God's ownership and "resemblance" with the eternal high priest. These are aspects that the Council of Trent emphasized in confrontation with the Reformers (cf *NR* 357, 514, 542; *DS* 1515, 1609, 1624; see also Ott 425f). In more recent Catholic baptismal teaching, by contrast, the main accent has been moved to two other aspects which belong as well to an old theological tradition but were largely ignored in the anti-Reformation controversy, e.g., the aspects of *incorporation* or reception into the faith community (cf *NR* 528; *DS* 1314,

632), and of the beginning of a personal *faith-history* which is supported by that community.

From this vantage point, baptism is seen completely in its *ecclesial dimension* in which the faith community is understood as the support of all personal faith-life. In the case of adult baptism (and contemporary theology takes this original form of the sacrament more and more into its considerations), the baptismal candidate is confronted with a profession of faith, a *Credo*, which is handed-down common property of the Church and, as such, challenges him to a personal decision of faith. If he decides to accept this Creed of the Church as truth which is for him existentially relevant, he enters the fellowship of the faithful, the *communis fidelium*, entrusts himself to this fellowship, and allows himself to be guided by it in the ethical consequences of his faith. This he does not out of an "individual and private 'ideology'" (*KuS* 78), but on the authority of the faith of the community which existed before him and in whose context he makes this faith his own by requesting the sacrament of baptism. In the case of an infant who is brought to baptism by others,[1] this occurs in a prior and anticipatory form; the gracious self-communication of God occurs as a "prevenient grace," and the confession of faith is made for the child vicariously by his parents and sponsors. It is said that the child is baptized "in the faith of the community" (*in fide ecclesiae*). Still, the entire process is directed toward a personal decision-making process in which the maturing individual takes a position for or against the Church and its Creed; and this decision is made not only once, as for example at the festive occasion of confirmation, but again and again until the end of one's life, in exactly the same way as the one baptized in adulthood. Baptism is here seen not only as a "permanent sacrament" but also as the beginning of a history which must be experienced in the on-going tension between personal existence and membership in the community.

All of this encompasses the term "initiation" which the newer baptismal theories and the Council (esp *SC* 69/1; *LG*

11/1; 31/1; *AG* 15/4) have again placed at the center of their reflection. This not only shows a conformity with the Pauline teaching on Christian initiation, but can be seen as well within the scope of an Augustinian-Thomistic systematic as the prime and immediate effect of the sacrament of baptism from which all further effects derive.[2] All other fruits—such as reconciliation, removal of guilt, healing and freeing for service of God and people—are mediated through the gift of initiation and its historically on-going development.

The same concept of a fundamental reference to the faith community resulting in a personal and active commitment is expressed in those speculations in which the Thomistic theory of "baptismal character" is combined with the New Testament motive of the "universal priesthood" of believers (cf 1 Pet 2:4-10; Rev 1:6; 5:9-10; 20:6). In this context, the "sign" is not merely a seal on the individual soul that one is known by and belongs to God; neither is it the certainty that the human individual becomes conformed to the image of the heavenly high priest in the divine ritual. Primarily it indicates one's membership in the great priestly collective of God's people and so an "ordination" and commitment to the task of service for God and man. Schillebeeckx formulates this concept in that he begins with the Thomistic thesis of the ecclesial community as "cult community" (*ChSG* 160), and then defines the commitment established by the character of baptism and confirmation as a "participation in the ritual and apostolic Father-cult of Christ" (*ChSG* 170). The Council's Dogmatic Constitution on the Church emphasizes, in the one text where sacramental "character" is mentioned, even more strongly the aspect of common faith-witness and apostolate:

> The sacred nature and organic structure of the priestly community is brought into operation through the sacraments and the exercise of virtue. Incorporated into the Church by baptism, the faithful are appointed by their baptismal character to Christian worship; reborn

as sons of God, they must profess before men the faith
they have received from God through the Church. By
the sacrament of confirmation they are more perfectly
bound to the Church and are endowed with the special
strength of the Holy Spirit. Hence they are, as true
witnesses of Christ, more strictly obliged to spread the
faith by word and deed (*LG* 11/1; cf *AG* 15/1).

In this context, the definition of the same Constitution
concerning the *laity* is remarkable:

The term "laity" is here understood to mean all the
faithful...who by baptism are incorporated into Christ,
are placed in the people of God, and in their own way
share the priestly, prophetic and kingly office of Christ,
and to the best of their ability carry on the mission of the
whole Christian people in the Church and in the world
(*LG* 31/1).

That is no other than the "apostolate of the laity" to which
all Christians are "appointed" through baptism and
confirmation, a "sharing in the salvific mission of the
Church" which is able to make of the various peoples "salt of
the earth" (*LG* 33/2) and to "contribute to the sanctification
of the world, as from within like leaven" (*LG* 31/2).

3.1.2. Paul's Reference to Christ and Spirit

The reading of such texts as have just been quoted may
give rise to the question whether the newer theology of
baptism does not place too much emphasis on its ecclesiolo-
gically centered context, whether it does not go too far in its
reaction against a certain individualism and ritualism, and
finally—and most crucially—whether it does not take the
activity of God and Christ less into its consideration than
does the more traditional Scholastic theology.

It could be answered that the Council's texts certainly

place the reality of "community," i.e., of the "people of God," at the center; but in doing so it is making use of that freedom to become one-sided which every reform movement and every attempted answer of the Church to challenges from without assumes as granted by an unwritten law of history. Indeed, even dogmatic definitions are "one-sided." Still, the suspicion that the Council is "ecclesiocentric" in its pronouncements on baptism is hardly cogent. Many of them are characterized, for example, by a determined desire to begin with the oldest baptismal accounts of the New Testament and so to re-emphasize the original *Christological* and *pneumatological* perspectives of Christian initiation—that is, to re-establish these perspectives in the face of their absence in Scholastic theology.[3]

The age-old conception, formulated by Paul, of the *historical community* of the baptized with the crucified, risen, and glorified Christ becomes sufficiently evident. The Constitution on the Sacred Liturgy states in connection with Romans 6, and with a touch of Casel's mystery theology: "Thus by baptism men are grafted into the paschal mystery of Christ; they die with him, are buried with him, and rise with him" (*SC* 6/1, with reference to Rom 6:4; Eph 2:6; Col 3:1; 2 Tim 2:11). And subsequently: "They received the spirit of adoption as sons 'in which we cry, Abba, Father' (Rom 8:15) and thus become true adorers such as the Father seeks." This Constitution does indeed tend toward a still stronger mystery-theological interpretation of Romans 6 (a fact that surely did not go without criticism by a strong group of modern exegetes),[4] but emphasizes no less strongly the essential relationship of the sacrament to Christ and the Spirit:

> Through baptism we are formed in the likeness of Christ: "For in one Spirit we are all baptized into one body" (1 Cor 12:13). In this sacred rite fellowship in Christ's death and resurrection is symbolized and is brought about: "For we were buried with him by means of baptism into death"; and if "we have been united with

him in the likeness of his death, we shall be so in the
likeness of his resurrection also" (Rom 6:4-5) (*LG* 7/2; cf
UR 22/1 with quotes from Col 2:12).

The expressions "in the likeness of" and "united with,"
which give a mystic and Platonic impression, are not
without their exegetical problems when the original Greek
text is used instead of its Latin translation (the Vulgate).
Paul did not mean a uniting of the baptismal candidate with
a replica, with a ritual replay of the Christ-event, but rather
with the living person of the once crucified and now
eternally contemporary Christ. This is the meaning of those
impressive verbal expressions used here and in similar
context by the apostle and his disciples: "crucified with,"
"buried with," "died with," "risen with," "living with," and
"reigning with" (Rom 6:4; Eph 2:6; Col 3:1; 2 Tim 2:11). These
expressions have to do with a mysterious, existential and
historical fellowship with Christ and his faith community
which extends to the ethical imperatives of Christian living
and takes on, therefore, a high degree of existential reality. It
is, of course, always the sovereign and free God who takes
the initiative in self-communication.

Paul's discussion of the *Holy Spirit* as the active agent
in baptism has a similar conceptual content. Wherever the
Council refers to the Spirit in its documents, it demonstrates
its desire to present the Spirit, who has been "sent into" the
life of the baptized, scripturally as the power of the "new
creation" (e.g., expressly in *GE* 8/1) which makes possible
and reasonable a uniquely intimate relationship to God
(expressed in the cry, "Abba, Father") and a close union with
fellow Christians (illustrated in the "one body"). When the
role of the creative Spirit of God is so strongly emphasized,
any discussion of an arbitrary concept of baptism on the
part of the Church becomes superfluous. The sacrament of
initiation does lead into the Church, but is, in the last
analysis, no "work" of the Church. In its basic dynamic it is
a work of the triune God in whose name it is administered.

3.1.3. Ecumenical Openness

It is just this emphasis in the theological statements of the Council, in pointing up the activity of Christ and the Spirit—an activity which transcends all purely human efforts—that lends considerable ecumenical perspective. This sort of "relativizing" in the sociological and ecclesiological aspects of a theology of baptism allows the confessional boundaries to appear less divisive.

It is significant that the most comprehensive texts of the Council concerning baptism appear in the Decree on Ecumenism. At the beginning of its first chapter, this document points to the new understanding that the use of the sacrament of baptism in its originally intended sense by the various Christian churches is the deciding factor of that unity which, in spite of all divisions, basically unites them with each other:

> After being lifted up on the cross and glorified, the Lord Jesus poured forth the Spirit whom he had promised, and through whom he has called and gathered together the people of the new covenant, which is the Church, into a unity of faith, hope and charity, as the apostle teaches us: "There is one body and one Spirit, just as you were called to the one hope of your calling: one Lord, one faith, one baptism" (Eph 4:4-5). For "all you who have been baptized into Christ have put on Christ...for you are all one in Christ Jesus" (Gal 3:27-28). It is the Holy Spirit, dwelling in those who believe and pervading and ruling over the entire Church, who brings about that wonderful communion of the faithful and joins them together so intimately in Christ that he is the principle of the Church's unity. By distributing various kinds of spiritual gifts and ministries, he enriches the Church of Jesus Christ with different functions "in order to equip the saints for the work of service, so as to build up the body of Christ" (Eph 4:12) (*UR* 2/2).

This text, which places baptism, in its clearly Christological and pneumatological perspective, at the sacramental focal point of ecclesial unity and points up the "various kinds of gifts and ministries" testifies not only to the exegetical honesty of its authors. It allows as well the assumption that the Council may be considering the possibility that the diversity in the understanding of dogmatic and ecclesial tradition, which caused and perpetuates the rupture between denominations, could, in the future, be transformed into variegated building blocks of the one body of Christ. If this interpretation is accurate, an implicit encouragement of further discussion could be seen, a consideration of the possibility that the emphases of the Reformers could have a charismatic element (i.e. given by the Spirit) just as those of the Catholic Church. Freed of the obstacles of error and destructive one-sidedness, these elements could contribute to that richness, to that colorful multiplicity in unity, at which the one baptism in the one Spirit aims.

Still, apart from such possible conclusions, the intention of the Council to make baptism the basis for interconfessional fraternity is clear:

> For men who believe in Christ and have been properly baptized are put in some, though imperfect, communion with the Catholic Church....It remains true that all who have been justified by faith in baptism are incorporated into Christ; they therefore have a right to be called Christians, and with good reason are accepted as brothers by the children of the Catholic Church (*UR* 3/1).[5]

The demands made by the fact of this baptism with respect to a progressive enlightening, deepening, and perfecting of the faith-life (both personally and inter-ecclesially) are shown by the following declaration:

> Baptism, therefore, constitutes the sacramental bond of unity existing among all who through it are reborn. But baptism, of itself, is only a beginning, a point of

departure, for it is wholly directed toward the acquiring of fullness of life in Christ. Baptism is thus ordained toward a complete profession of faith, a complete incorporation into the system of salvation such as Christ himself willed it to be, and finally, toward a complete integration into eucharistic communion (*UR* 22/2; cf 4, 10).

Here the goal appears to be the acceptance of the creed without reservation, and the participation in the sacraments, whose pinnacle is the Eucharist, without hindrance. Still, such "objective" demands can hardly supplant the notion of an equally necessary and fundamental encounter—as difficult as this may be to determine "objectively"—between the proclaimed *word of God* and the individual who is being called to faith by it. There are sufficient texts in the Council documents in which the proclamation of the word is indicated as being the all-inclusive moment (apart from which the sacraments would practically be powerless) in which salvation is communicated. This most certainly complies with certain concerns of the Reformation. Of those texts which, with emphasis, mention "the word" *before* the sacrament, only a few from the Decree on the Church's Missionary Activity need be mentioned (*AG* 6/3; 7/1; 9/2). Here the new birth through the word of God (cf 1 Pet 1:23) is spoken of before mention is made of incorporation into the Church through baptism. It is also stated that the Christian must be nourished by the word of God as well as by the eucharistic bread. In this way, that faith which is necessary for salvation is awakened and kept alive. Regarding the "means of grace" which are "necessary" for salvation because they are willed by Christ, the faith of the individual which is awakened by the word, the sacraments which are celebrated by the faith community, and the Church itself, which is the "body of Christ," are all mentioned in one breath, and their reciprocal effectiveness is alluded to. In this way, baptism appears in the comprehensive context of a communicative economy of grace.

3.2. Confirmation

Actually, the second of the seven sacraments should not be treated separately at all, but should find its proper place within a single baptism-confirmation complex. Indeed, the most recent Catholic theology emphasizes for this sacrament its great "proximity to baptism as a part of Christian initiation" (*KuS* 46). The structural and functional unity of both moments of initiation are discussed, whereby baptism retains its foundational, deciding, and primary role. This is referred to as being "two sacramental phases of an essential single...process" (*KuS* 48) which could be temporally separated from each other—but not necessarily; or baptism and confirmation are seen as a single Christian "ritual of initiation with two sacramental focal points" (*ChSG* 164). The close unity and reciprocal relationship of these two ritual acts has already been discussed in Chapter Two.

It must be admitted, however, that the Council of Trent set the accent differently in that it taught, in contrast to the denial of the sacramentality of confirmation by the Reformers, that this ritual act is a "true and actual sacrament" (*NR* 555; *DS* 1628). The special position, peculiarity, and autonomy of this second sacrament was further emphasized in that the Council, in connection with the "decree for the Armenians" from the year 1439, gave the role of its "proper minister" to the "bishop alone" (*NR* 557; *DS* 1630; cf *NR* 553; *DS* 1138). It should be noted, however, that Vatican II provided a "corrective" to this teaching by making the bishop the "original minister of confirmation" (*minister originarius confirmationis*) in order not to be in the position of rejecting the Oriental church practice in which every priest normally administers this sacrament (*LG* 26/3; cf *OE* 13f).

The pre- and post-Tridentine theology, which sought to legitimatize confirmation as an autonomous sacrament, found for it no specific "word of institution" by Jesus (insofar as his promise to send the Spirit was not considered in this context); but it did find an apostolic foundation. The apostles Peter and John were sent to Samaria, where those already baptized by the missionary Philip had, surprisingly enough, not yet received the Holy Spirit. There they conferred the gift of the Spirit in that they "imposed hands on them" (Acts 8:14-17). This was now interpreted as an "indirect proof" of the institution of the sacrament of confirmation by Christ. Such attempts at legitimation, or other similar ones,[6] cannot stand up under a scientific exegesis. Nor did the ecclesial practice of the first two and a half centuries offer any evidence for a systematic differentiation—K. Rahner speaks of a "splitting apart of" (*KuS* 46)—between baptism and confirmation. This kind of thinking is first seen by Cyprian,[7] who characteristically used the above mentioned Samaria-episode to find a legitimation for the communication of the gift of the Spirit, the sealing and "perfecting" of the baptized, through the imposition of the bishop's hands.

After Cyprian, there is considerable variation among the patristic witnesses concerning the sense of this episcopal intervention in the initiation process. The delegates to the Synod of Elvira (ca. A.D. 303) were content to demand that in case a believer, because of a serious illness, received an "emergency baptism" from a layman or was baptized by a deacon, the rite should subsequently be "completed" (*perficere*) through the imposition of hands or the blessing of the bishop (*DS* 120f). This rite was not referred to as "confirmation" and was only intended for exceptional situations. In any case, the Synod of Elvira points in the same direction as the Samaria account in Acts: the highest ecclesial authority is responsible for the proper functioning of the initiation process, has authority to supervise it and—if nothing stands in the way—to bless it. What is here evident is the great seriousness with which the primitive Church approached the *catechumenate*: baptism should be well prepared and followed up, and it must lead into a developing faith-life which is supported by the faith community and supervised by the bishop.

Jerome testifies to a rite of the imposition of hands

which immediately followed the rite of baptism and was intended as an invocation of the Holy Spirit. He emphasizes, however, quite specifically that the Spirit had already been totally given in baptism (*Dial. c. Luciferanos* 8; *PL* 23, 163f). Augustine, on the other hand, tended rather to reserve this communication of the Spirit to the "consummation" of initiation by the bishop (*Sermo* 269; *PL* 38, 1235). Cyril of Jerusalem speaks of an "anointing" which opens to the baptized the true "gnosis" that is in possession of the Spirit. Whoever receives this anointing is made capable of a bold witness of faith. In passing it can be noted that Cyril had his problems with the Samaria-episode; he does not comprehend why the missionary Philip, who was himself endowed with the Spirit (as were all of the seven "Greeks" ordained by the apostles to special service), had to defer the communication of the Spirit to Peter and John.[8] John Chrysostom answered this question with a curiously "episcopal" explanation in which he claims that only the Twelve and their successors, the bishops, have the privilege of conferring the "Spirit of the symbols" (*Homily* 18; *PG* 60, 143f). In the following period, the interpretation of the Acts passage remained determinative. Nearly all of the Greek Fathers after Chrysostom ascribe the privilege of "completing" the baptismal ritual and "perfecting" baptismal grace to apostolic authority. From this, the Western Scholasticism of the Middle Ages deduced the exclusive right of the bishop. He alone is entitled to apply the holy oil of confirmation and to validly bestow confirmation, being its "proper minister." Since the twelfth century then, the rite, which was generally referred to as "confirmation," was considered by all of the various Scholastic theological schools of thought as an actual sacrament, the second of the seven.

The more precise determination of the efficacy of this rite was expressed by the above mentioned Decree for the Armenians (1439). This stated: "Through confirmation grace is multiplied and our faith is strengthened." And again:

> The efficacy of this sacrament consists of the strength-
> ening by the Holy Spirit which it confers, just as it was
> given to the apostles on Pentecost, so that the Christian
> can confess the name of Christ with courage (*NR* 502,
> 554; *DS* 1311, 1319).

The catechism, which was written in the spirit of the Council
of Trent, refers to another aspect, i.e., that of the specific
effect of confirmation in the completion of baptismal grace
(*Cat. Rom.* II 3, 19). Certain of the modern Scholastics reflect
in various forms once again the Thomistic thesis that
confirmation impresses a second "indelible sign" upon the
soul in order to arm the individual for struggle against the
enemies of faith, to conform him to the image of Christ as
teacher of the truth, king of justice and high priest, and to
commit him to an open profession of his Christian faith (cf
STh III 72, 5).

Current theological thought has a different point of
departure to that of the Middle Ages, but it holds firmly to
one point of tradition: the meaning of confirmation is
ultimately to be found in the safeguarding of that *mission* in
Church and world which is already grounded in baptism (cf
KuS 82; *ChSG* 165). This commitment to missionary activity
certainly no longer has the aggressive implications of a
"perfected soldier of Christ" standing against unbelievers.
But it does have to do with a conviction of faith that is of
high quality, characterized by a sense of responsibility and a
willingness to act and give witness, and which can be
realized only in the power of the *Holy Spirit*. The fact that
confirmation originated from the official intervention of
Church authority, which was designated to control and
validate the sacrament of baptism, appears today to be of
secondary importance. What really counts is the context of
the well-ordered and active *faith community* in which the
mission, which is effectively supported by confirmation, is to
be carried out.

The meaning of confirmation can today be made plain

in the context of these points of emphasis which have developed as a consequence of an earnest consideration of the meaning of infant baptism. In infant baptism, seen in isolation, the essence of the sacrament as encounter between the Church's proclamation of Christ's offer of salvation and the faith of the believer, who is willing to participate in the life of Christ, certainly does not come to fruition. To baptize an infant means to temporally anticipate the later fulfillment of this essence, but does not supersede it. So it is that every baptized individual, as he matures, must make the personal decision to accept or reject his baptism. When a young Christian in a free act of faith—which, of course, necessitates religious formation—ratifies the fact of his being Christian, the situation occurs in which confirmation becomes completely meaningful. This second sacramental focal point of the one process of Christian initiation can best be understood as the perfecting or fulfilling of baptism, which otherwise would remain in its full sense imperfect and merely anticipated in the individual life-history. Therefore, one of the strongest moments of legitimation for the celebration of confirmation is to be found in the common practice of infant baptism. Because infant baptism—in contrast to the practice in the primitive Church—is now the norm, it must be ratified, perfected, "confirmed" so that it can become, not only in theory, but in practice, the foundation of a personal conviction of faith which gives rise to apostolic activity. It is then clear that this "confirmation" of baptism becomes simultaneously a concern of one's own conscience, of the Holy Spirit, and of the co-responsible faith community and its leader, who administers the rite.

Vatican II shows its awareness of this fact. This became clear when it emphasized (following the lead of modern research) not so much the autonomy of the sacrament of confirmation as its radical connection with Christian initiation which is basically grounded in baptism and constantly renewed through participation in the Eucharist (*AG* 11/1; 14/2; 36/1; cf *OE* 13f). With a consistent liturgical concreteness, the Council emphasizes the fundamental unity of, and the functional relationship between, baptism and confirmation:

> The rite of confirmation is to be revised also so that the intimate connection of this sacrament with the whole of the Christian initiation may more closely appear. For this reason the renewal of baptismal promises should fittingly precede the reception of this sacrament (*SC* 71/1).

What does this renewal of baptismal promises say other than emphasize that free act of faith by which the young Christian, who is now capable of such decision, ratifies his baptism and the apostolic commitment connected with it?

Regarding the *effectiveness* of confirmation, the Council indicates, in a series of comparatives, that it has to do with an unfolding of that which is grounded in baptism:

> By the sacrament of confirmation they are more perfectly bound to the Church and are endowed with a special strength of the Holy Spirit. Hence they are, as true witnesses of Christ, more strictly obliged to spread the faith by word and deed (*LG* 11/1).

And the Decree on the Apostolate of Lay People states especially well how this unfolding of baptismal grace in the life of the individual is to take place in the context of the three sacraments of initiation:

> From the fact of their union with Christ the head flows the laymen's right and duty to be apostles. Inserted as they are in the mystical body of Christ by baptism and strengthened by the power of the Holy Spirit in confirmation, it is by the Lord himself that they are assigned to the apostolate....Charity, which is, as it were, the soul of the whole apostolate, is given to them and nourished in them by the sacraments, the Eucharist above all (*AA* 3/1).

These theoretical sounding but praxis oriented statements raise, of course, the psychological question as to the *right age* for confirmation. In this respect, research has been quite diverse. The pastoral theologian R. Zerfa summarizes the main streams of thought as follows:

> In the first case...the confirmation theology of "decision," which has developed in the West, is taken seriously, and the deduction is made, as a result, to confirm only young adults—even at the risk that only few will be confirmed. In the second case, leave is taken of this theology with a flippancy that astonishes the laity, and recourse is taken toward the ancient Church practice of a baptism-confirmation-Eucharist sequence. This occurs with the help of a completely new (or very old) theology of initiation.... Thought through consistently, this approach leads to the Oriental church practice of confirming infants.[9]

It is clear that the latter is no real solution and that the still widespread practice of confirming six- to ten-year-olds cannot do justice to the high standards set by the Council. It would certainly be in keeping with the basic intention of the Council and its contingent apostolic perspective to demand, in any case, an earnest process of conscious formation as a prerequisite for the commitment implicit in confirmation. Otherwise, sacramental praxis would neglect to take the reality of our social context into consideration.

3.3. The Eucharist

No sacrament in the course of history has experienced such an extensive analysis and explanation as the cultic mystery of the Lord's Supper; and no other sacrament, ironically, has so often been the cause of theological and confessional strife as this *sacramentum unitatis*. It has only been in the last few years, for example, that the hefty discussion has slackened concerning how the real presence of Christ in the eucharistic celebration comes about.[10] And at present, considerable hindrances from the side of canon law, the teaching office, and so-called systematic theology resist the practice of the common celebration of the Last Supper among Christians of various denominations, i.e., "inter-Communion."[11]

In the narrow confines of this introduction, not even the main streams of the current discussion of the Eucharist can be presented. Even if this were possible, it is by no means certain that the many suggested solutions would not confuse more than lead to the core of the sacrament. It would seem then more helpful first of all to trace the great traditional themes of Catholic eucharistic teaching, primarily as they are presented by the Council of Trent, and then to discuss the shift in emphasis and the new accents set for this dogmatic tradition by Vatican II in its double endeavor to remain loyal to the origins and at the same time to do justice to current thought. In fact, this latest ecumenical Council did reshape a number of areas, and in so doing either quietly confirmed certain directons in theological research or encouraged their continued pursuit.

3.3.1. Central Points of Emphasis in Traditional Doctrine

What Jesus intended in the symbolic action of his "Last Supper," and what form the words, prayers, and instructions included in this act had, can only be grasped in the light of the worship and proclamation practiced in the primitive Church. The four "Last Supper accounts" of Mark, Matthew, Luke, and Paul are the sole primary sources of the tradition that makes this intention of Jesus understandable as it was celebrated after his death by his disciples, celebrated in fraternal fellowship around the table as they called upon his name, hoping for the coming of God's kingdom as they were being nourished by the Spirit of God. It is true that each of the four witnesses was influenced by his own faith-community, and so the proclamation content contains distinct moments of interpretation. But still, three common theological motives are identifiable: (a) the proclamation, that brings to mind the death of Jesus, in which the liturgical symbols themselves have *memoria*-character; (b) the consciousness, that this memorial meal has an effect upon the participants around the table—here and now—in which they are reconciled by Jesus' self-sacrifice and confirmed as members of his "new covenant"; (c) the expectancy, that is fitting for all disciples of Jesus, in which they await in hope his victorious return in the "kingdom of the Father."[12]

A fourth common motive could be mentioned, that of "thanksgiving," from which the Eucharist takes its name. According to all four accounts, the Eucharist has its origin in the word of thanksgiving spoken by Jesus at the beginning of the celebration.[13] These motives are scattered throughout the patristic teachings of East and West, whereas they are systematized in the high Scholasticism of the Middle Ages (cf Thomas, *STh* III 60, 3).

The hefty controversies within Western theology between the "realist" and "symbolic" schools of the Augustinian heritage concerned almost exclusively the "sacrament of the altar," as the Lord's Supper came to be called in the context of cultic sacrificial terminology. The discussion became polarized around a single main question: How is it possible for the body and blood of the once crucified Christ, who is now glorified and living in heaven, to be really and effectually present in the sacramental "elements" of bread and wine? Or, seen from another perspective: What quality inheres in the host (the problem of the chalice became increasingly secondary) which, after the priest's words of consecration, lies on the altar and is presented for adoration to the faithful? The doctrine of the "real presence" developed which, of course, was interpreted and explained variously according to theological perspective and style of spirituality. This doctrine long became the prime test of orthodoxy in the controversy (even within the Reformation!)

concerning sacraments. All other aspects of the eucharistic mystery were subordinated to this one. Only the question concerning the sacrificial character of the Mass was able to challenge, for a time (i.e., in the post-Tridentine apologetic against the denial of the atoning efficacy of the Eucharist by the Reformation), the predominance of the question concerning the real presence. Such over-development of a doctrinal aspect, which for the primitive Church and ancient Church tradition presented no real problem for their Christian sacramental understanding, can certainly not be simply rejected as a sign of decadence. It was the result of a need on the part of the faithful to have the closest possible contact with the glorified Christ. This may indeed have wavered between a selfless and loving mysticism and a desire to have Christ "at hand" for one's own use. For the majority, the common denominator was certainly the wish for "contact with Christ."

3.3.1.1. The Real Presence

When one opens a book of Scholastic dogmatics, the result of this doctrinal development becomes clear in that the theme of the real presence is treated before the other two "classical" themes of sacrament and sacrifice. After a short treatment of the "heretical antitheses" (Ott)—which extend from an anti-sacramentalism that is opposed to the corporeal and material, to a mystical spiritualism and an enlightened rationalism—the Tridentine defense of the Catholic faith-tradition is given:

> Whoever denies that in the sacrament of the Holy Eucharist the soul and divinity of our Lord Jesus Christ and consequently the entire Christ is truly, really and essentially embodied, as if he were present only in sign, image, or efficacy, he is excluded (*NR* 577; *DS* 1651).

Contemporary thinkers who prefer a personalistic

approach may find strange the "additive" character of this line of thought, in which the "entire Christ" seems to be a product of the several component parts. However, a closer observation and examination of the text shows that its basic intention is no other than a Christological realism as represented in the Gospel of John; the Eucharist deserves the name "bread of life" only because it is the sacrament of the living and life-giving Christ. Indeed, the Council quotes as scriptural proof John 6:57: "The man who feeds on me will have life because of me" (cf *NR* 570; *DS* 1638). Here the Johannine Jesus identifies himself with the "bread that came down from heaven," which corresponds to the "this is my body" of the Last Supper account.

The Council of Trent did not stop at this clear adherence to the mysterious but nonetheless real identity of the living and powerfully active Christ with the sacramentally present Christ. It was not satisfied with a clarification of the faith-reality—which ultimately is the concern of the communicant alone—that in the Eucharist there occurs a deeply personal encounter of the aspirant, who is seeking life, with the life-giving Lord. The Council sees itself obliged by certain challenges of the Reformers to address a problem which appears to be quite technical, that of the metaphysical (or even physical) constitution of the *bread*, which becomes body, and of the *wine*, which becomes blood. The terminology used for this is largely Aristotelian; it speaks of a transformation of "substances" along with unchanging "forms."

> Through the consecration of bread and wine there occurs a transformation of the entire substance of bread into the substance of the body of Christ, our Lord, and of the entire substance of the wine into the substance of his blood. And this transformation is properly called by the Catholic Church and is in actuality a transubstantiation (*NR* 572; *DS* 1642; cf *NR* 578; *DS* 1652).

The technicality, which is so introduced, goes so far as to speak of the presence of Christ in the individual particles of the elements and of the treatment of the bread fragments which are left over after Communion.

Concering the *nature* of the real presence which occurs through "transubstantiation," it is described as "total," permanent, and *worthy of adoration* (cf. *NR* 579-583; *DS* 1653-1657). What is meant is that the Christ, who is present in his incarnate totality in all the particles of the sacramental elements, remains present after the completion of the actual eucharistic celebration and is to be "adored with all the acts of homage proper to the worship of God." And so all of those pious customs, such as Corpus Christi processions and eucharistic devotions which arose in the Middle Ages, receive—now aimed against the Reformers—their doctrinal confirmation.

3.3.1.2. As Sacrament

Only the above mentioned historical development and theological controversy can explain why the dogmatic handbooks treat the sacramentality of the Eucharist after the question of the real presence, and methodologically apart from it. And it is also conspicuous that the statements concerning this secondary thematic complex do not bear the same degree of certainty as those formulations concerning the real presence. Only those legitimizing statements concerning the institution, the necessary "material," the saving efficacy, the legitimacy of Communion under the form of bread alone, and the minister and communicant of the "valid sacrament" (cf Ott 467, 473f, 475) bear the label *"de fide,"* i.e., are understood as having the greatest binding authority for Christian faith. On the other hand, the formulations concerning the efficacy, which is the goal of the Eucharist in its total sacramentality, an efficacy based on biblical testimony, are only qualified with the third degree of certainty (i.e., *sententiae certae*). The reason for this is not necessarily to be found in a loss of ability to differentiate between the essential and the non-essential. It is to be found rather in the simple fact that this aspect of efficacy in Catholic tradition was never seriously questioned by false teaching. (This is, by the way, a good example to make clear the function of the dogmatic "degree of certainty": The "highest" are not necessarily given to the self-evident truths and to those which ecclesial tradition has considered as particularly important, but to those which have been most discussed or controverted.) Nonetheless, it can be justly lamented that the traditional doctrine of the efficacy of the Lord's Supper does not stand at the beginning of the Scholastic tracts.

Three goals of eucharistic efficacy have been formulated in the Decree for the Armenians: community with Christ, community of Christians with each other, and the spiritual strengthening of the individual. The following is declared:

> The efficacy of this sacrament in the soul of its worthy recipient is the union of the human individual with Christ. Since, however, the individual is incorporated into the body of Christ and made one with his members through grace, the result is that this grace is multiplied in the worthy communicant of this sacrament; and every effect that physical food and drink has for the material body—they preserve, enhance, renew and delight—this sacrament effects for the spiritual body (*NR* 566; *DS* 1322).

Both of the first mentioned aspects of efficacy have clear witness in the New Testament. For the first, John 6:56: "The man who feeds on my flesh and drinks my blood remains in me, and I in him." And for the second, 1 Corinthians 10:17: "Because the loaf of bread is one, we, many though we are, are one body, for we all partake of the one loaf." The symbolic interpretation, which was widespread in the ancient Church, of the many grains of wheat and the many grapes that become a unity in bread and wine, points in the same direction.[14] Similarly, Augustine speaks of a growing incorporation into the unity of the body of Christ, of a "sign of unity" and a "bond of love."[15] The third aspect of efficacy mentioned repeats an aspect of Thomistic reflection concerning the efficacy of the sacrament in its life-forming goal of both biological and sacramental nourishment, a doctrinal aspect of that theological anthropology that makes much of Thomas' thinking appealing even today (cf *STh* III 79, 1-6; summarized in Ott 471f).

A fourth and not less scriptural goal of the efficacy in the "sacrament of ecclesial unity" (Thomas) is suggested by the Council of Trent itself, namely the *eschatological* goal. Although the Council neglected to see that, according to the Synoptic Gospels, Jesus points to a future celebration of the Eucharist (according to Mt 26:29) together with his disciples in the "kingdom of his Father" (cf Mk 14:25; Lk 22:16), it did not neglect—probably with reference to John 6:54—to give space to the individual perspective of eschatological hope. It declares that the Eucharist is a "pledge of our future glory and unending bliss" (*NR* 570; *DS* 1638). So the sacrament appears to be an ever repeatable anticipation of the resurrection life, the actual material hope of the Christian faithful.

3.3.1.3. As Sacrifice

In contrast to the most crucial and decisive objection of the Reformers, that the New Testament no longer knows a cultic sacrifice and nowhere designates the Lord's Supper as such, the Council of Trent declares emphatically:

> Whoever says that in the Mass God is not presented with a true and actual sacrifice, or that the sacrificial act consists in the fact alone that Christ is presented to us as food, he is excluded (*NR* 606; *DS* 1751).

When the argumentation is considered that leads to this conclusion, it becomes clear that the Tridentine fathers were not satisfied with arguing from an extra-biblical tradition (cf Ott 482f) of the first century in order to refute Luther.

They demonstrated rather an attempt to be open to the Lutheran criticism in their search for a biblical and Christ-centered substantiation for their position. At the very beginning of the first chapter of their Doctrine of the Holy Sacrifice of the Mass it becomes clear that the "true and actual sacrifice" that is presented to God "in the Mass" is understood fundamentally as the *one* sacrifice, the singular and unique self-offering of Jesus Christ. The first scriptural proof for this the Council took, strangely enough, not from the words of institution with their allusions to the sacrifice of the old covenant (cf Ex 24:8) which designated the elements of the Lord's Supper with traditional sacrificial terminology of the "body to be given for you" and the "blood which will be shed for you" (cf Lk 22:19-20), and placing this meal as a celebration of continual and renewed remembrance in the context of the command, "Do this in remembrance of me" (Lk 22:19; 1 Cor 11:24). If the Council of Trent had done so, it would possibly have found more understanding from the opposition party of the Reformation. For they held firmly as well to a mysterious but nonetheless real identity of the Christ, who had once offered himself, with the three separate forms in which he makes himself present, i.e., that it is the one and the same Christ who anticipated his redeeming self-sacrifice at the "Last Supper," completed it by his death on the cross, and makes it present for us ever and again in the celebration of the "Lord's Supper." Was it not Luther who taught that in this sense the fellowship of Jesus' disciples— then and now—could only "receive" the sacrificial merits of Christ's life, therefore making the celebration of the Lord's Supper solely a giving of thanks, i.e., "Eucharist"?

The Council chose instead a different means of proving the Christocentric existence of the sacrifice offered *in* the Mass. It took up the symbolic theology of the Letter to the Hebrews, which describes Christ as the permanent heavenly high priest (Heb 7-10). Because Christ is *the* eschatological priest of God, who alone is able to redeem and sanctify all men by a *single* and *unique* sacrifice, his self-sacrifice for the participants, which is actualized *in* the Mass, is a never ceasing access to salvation. The Council states:

> Thus our Lord and God did indeed intend to once offer himself to God the Father by his death on the altar of the cross in order to effect eternal redemption for all. Because, however, his priesthood was not to be obliterated by his death (Heb 7:24, 27), he desired at that last meal in the night of his betrayal to leave his beloved Bride, the Church, a visible sacrifice, as human nature requires, in which that bloody sacrifice, that was to be offered once upon the cross, is made present (*repraesentaretur*), preserves his memory (*memoria*) until the end of time, and applies (*applicaretur*) his healing power for the forgiveness of the sins which we daily commit (*NR* 597; *DS* 1740).

These last mentioned key terms—*repraesentatio, memoria, applicatio*—give the sense, goal, and function of that "visible sacrifice" which the Church received from Christ. It is to be the often repeated sacrament of the unique self-sacrifice, the one sacrifice of Jesus Christ. Through his sacramental existence, the eternally present high priest wills to make himself present, to memorialize himself, to heal and sanctify. Even when the texts themselves do not expressly develop the idea of the "Sacrifice of the Mass" as a *sacramental* sacrifice which ultimately derives from that "primary administrator" of all sacraments, still this corresponds to the impression given by the document as a whole. This is demonstrated by the weighty statement that appears further on:

> For it is one and the same sacrificial gift, and it is the same one, who at the time of the cross sacrificed himself, who now sacrifices through the ministry of the priest; alone the manner of offering is different. The fruits of that sacrifice, namely of the bloody one, are abundantly gained through this unbloody one; so the bloody

sacrifice is in no way through the unbloody diminished
(*NR* 599; *DS* 1734).

The apologetic phrase at the end of this quotation
betrays the chief objection of the Reformers; they held it for
blasphemy against the cross to wish to supplement it with
other, subsequent sacrificial acts, which were offered by
man and determined by his private religious interests. The
accusation that the many ecclesial Sacrifices of the Mass
presumptuously diminished the one sacrifice of Christ is
rejected by the Council of Trent. Still, its formulations
contain much which, in reference to this critical point, could
give the impression of inconsistency or falsehood in the eyes
of the Reformation party. So, for example, in spite of the
solemn assertion of the absolute uniqueness, unsurpassa-
bility, and eternal validity of the *sacerdotium* of Christ, still
the apostles and their successors are referred to as
sacerdotes. In addition, these priests appear to be in
themselves the subjects of the sacramental-sacrificial act,
similar to the priests of the old covenant, with whom, by the
way, they are placed in parallel, just as the "sacrifice of the
new covenant" (referring to the Mass) is to that of the old
(*NR* 597; *DS* 1740; cf *NR* 706; *DS* 1764). The concept develops
logically, then, that it is the priests of the Church who today
sacrifice Christ, whereby the work of Christ appears to be
reduced to the mere "appointment" of such sacrificial priests
in the Church. At least the following statement could be so
interpreted—with just a touch of intellectual mistrust:

> For after the celebration of the old paschal lamb...he
> [Jesus Christ] instituted the new paschal lamb himself
> so that he could be *sacrificed by the Church* through the
> priests under visible signs.

The fact that the Council asserted clearly—against the
Lutheran position that the Eucharist could be designated at
the most as a sacrifice of thanks and praise—that the
Sacrifice of the Mass "is" (*esse*), as a "visible sacrifice," "an

atoning sacrifice for the living and the dead" (the title of the second chapter: *NR* 599; *DS* 1743; cf *NR* 607; *DS* 1753) could very well have strengthened this misunderstanding. In addition, it is suggested that the priest has the authority to offer the sacrifice of reconciliation for the benefit of a particular individual, living or dead, for "reparation and for other needs," and further "to honor the saints and achieve their intercession" and at the same time that he can partake in Holy Communion together with others present or even completely alone; so the possibility is given that Christians of the Reformation, who objected to abuses of the late Middle Ages in just these areas, were not completely convinced by the otherwise Christocentric eucharistic teaching of the Council.

In fact, the Council of Trent was not able to offer a final clarification of this hotly disputed issue of sacrifice which was acceptable to all. In spite of its emphasis on the essentially relative character of the "eucharistic sacrifice" (Vatican II gave this term definite precedence over the designation "Sacrifice of the Mass"), and in spite of all stress on the radical dependency of the many Masses on the one sacrifice,[16] the Counter-Reformation Council left considerable room for speculation concerning the "physical" and "metaphysical" essence of the Sacrifice of the Mass, which was seen as a more or less autonomous "sacrifice of the Church" (cf Ott 485–489). Among the resulting post-Tridentine theories, the so-called destruction theories particularly strained the Christological sensitivity of Protestant Christians. These theories considered, for example, an actual destruction or alteration of the sacrificial gifts on the altar as a condition for the sacrificial sense of the Mass, or a transposition of the body and blood of Christ into the lower state of food and drink, or finally a mystical slaughtering of Christ by the sword of the words of consecration.

When one considers these excesses in Catholic eucharistic theology of the last four centuries and becomes conscious of their dangerous estrangement from—indeed opposition to—Scripture, when one takes into account the pastoral sterility of the resulting sacramental casuistry of the Mass, one learns to value highly the (still uninterpreted) Tridentine texts in their honest attempt to restore the Christ-centeredness of early Christianity and at the same time to protect the Eucharist from anti-sacramental tendencies. On the other hand, one notices with relief how very differently the problematic of the Eucharist is considered in present Catholic research and Vatican II.

3.3.2. Emphases of Contemporary Theology

A more recent Catholic theology of the Lord's Supper demonstrates a good example of return to the sources (biblical and patristic) and of orientation toward relevant experiential aspects of ecclesial existence. This is seen above all in the fact that the Scholastic order of precedence—real presence, sacrament, sacrifice—has changed to an approach in which the *communal aspects* (one could also say the *communio*-essence) of the eucharistic sacrament is given the function of a hermeneutic middle. This means primarily considering every line central which can be traced from the practice of the historical Jesus in fellowship with his disciples at table, by way of Paul's one-body theory and the Augustinian-Thomistic caritas theory, to the decisions of the teaching office concerning the eucharistic union of the faithful with and in Christ. All other aspects of the *sacramentum unitas,* including the aspects of sacrifice and real presence, are seen and interpreted from this central point. The conviction predominates among theologians with more or less clarity that the finality of the Lord's Supper lies in the enabling of fellowship with Christ and with Christians. *In order that* this two-dimensional *communio* become an experienceable reality, Christ, according to this concept, makes himself *present*, in spite of all spatial-temporal distance, and unfolds the reconciling and unifying power of his singular and unique *sacrifice*. Real presence and sacrifice are, so to speak, at the service of the encounter of God with the human individual and of individuals with each other; neither the real presence nor the eucharistic sacrifice of Christ is seen as an end in itself. Earlier speculation, by no means irrelevant, that the Sacrifice of the Mass is an ecclesial-priestly act in order to "produce" the real presence of Christ in tabernacle and monstrance, and to present him to the community of faith for adoration, no longer finds a place in more modern theology. Nor does a ritual casuistry that thought itself capable of differentiating between the essential and unessential in eucharistic celebration.

In these new approaches, which emphasize the centrality of community, emphasis is indeed given, as already mentioned, to inter-personal exchange in the eucharistic celebration, to an ability to experience and actively cooperate in this communication. Still, a particular brand of vulgar post-conciliar theology has sunk to the low level of a so-called horizontalism in which the Eucharist becomes merely an occasion for humanitarian or social critique and admonition. The authoritative reformers of Catholic eucharistic understanding never differentiate between an emphasis on the highest attainable level of communication and community experience, and a clear consciousness of the mystery of Christ who makes possible and sustains every such two-dimensional encounter. The variations and bases of these motives that have been formulated through theological and conciliar research will be exemplified in the next paragraphs.

3.3.2.1. Ecclesial Experience of Community

The mystery-theology of Odo Casel, whose central point was the eucharistic cult-mystery, contributed considerably to a rediscovery of the original aspects of participation, unity, and community at the heart of the eucharistic celebration. The point of departure, in order to theologically analyze it as such, was the liturgical celebration. The way led from the concrete experience to the theological expression of the mystery and not, as in the case of most neo-Scholastic tracts on the sacraments, from the abstract determination of essential structures to their casuistic-ritualistic realization. Because the celebration of the Eucharist was understood as the pinnacle of ecclesial existence—especially since the Church was primarily understood as cult-community, as the great family of those worshiping God—the accent was shifted, in theoretical reflections as well, to the efficacy of the sacrament in creating community. The Church appeared, then, not only as *the* corresponding point of encounter between the Easter-mystery and the cult-mystery, but also as that unity which is built up, strengthened, and grows through such moments of encounter.[17]

The intellectual atmosphere created by this mystery-theology contributed not only to a stimulation of patristic studies regarding the Eucharist in which those elements that had incorrectly been based on biblical and patristic texts became clear.[18] It contributed as well to a comprehensive systematic reflection, as above all in the case of Karl Rahner. It is true that Rahner, like other Catholic systematic theologians, invested much energy in the discussion of transubstantiation[19]—a fact that points up the specific problems that remained unresolved by the Council of Trent. Still, his main interest became increasingly the ecclesiological implications of the Lord's Supper. In his small but important book, *Church and Sacrament* (the title is itself an entire program), he declares:

> We begin not with baptism (as in the usual tracts on the sacraments), but with the Eucharist.... Without doubt the celebration of the Eucharist is an absolutely central act in the Church (*KuS* 73).

Not only *in* the Church, but *of* the Church. The eucharistic Communion is more than a private "consumption" of the body of Christ by the individual soul.

It is a becoming more deeply incorporated into the mystical body of Christ, since the Savior left his Church his real body as a sign of his unity and love, through which he desired to make all Christians conscious of their unity with each other (*KuS* 74). Rahner quotes here almost verbatim a formulation of the Council of Trent which, however, the Council itself did not emphasize as a central teaching (cf *NR* 567; *DS* 1635.)

Here the thought complex is central which includes the various elements of the Pauline *soma*-concept, the picture of the grains of wheat in the Didache, and the Augustinian and Thomistic doctrine of the *sacramentum unitatis*. Consequently, it is stated that the immediate effect of the Eucharist, which points to and results in all other effects, consists in the incorporation of the faithful into the body of Christ. This means that in each celebration of the Lord's Supper in which the participants take part with a commitment of faith, the Church, the collective body of Christ, is constituted. And this eucharistic constitution of the Church, this "becoming-the-body-of-Christ" of the participants, becomes an effective sign of grace. So it can be said that "the body of Christ is a sign of grace" (*KuS* 75).

Behind this consideration is, of course, Rahner's thesis of the Church as "original sacrament" of the eschatological self-communication of God in Christ. Because the Church, in its mystical essence, is the "original sacrament," and because all sacraments are essentially "self-expression" of the Church, the Eucharist appears as the highest self-expression of the Church and as comprehensive actualization of its original-sacramentality. For in this sacrament alone, the "original sacramental word" of God, Christ, makes himself savingly present in his total being. This presence signifies at the same time unity. And this unity in its greatest actuality is accomplished when the Church celebrates the Eucharist (cf *KuS* 75).

It could be objected here that this theory presupposes an *idealized* conception of the Church in its global totality and allows no room for the actual experience that the Church can also be—and often is—a hindrance for the self-revelation of God. Also the question of the concrete experience of unity, which is raised by the often frustrating and stereotyped manner in which the eucharistic liturgy is celebrated, is left untreated. Still, Rahner opens in this respect an important door in that he addresses the ecclesiological relevance of the eucharistic celebration in *local parishes*, "groups, and fraternities" (*KuS* 77). In fact, *the* Church of God is realized in the *concrete* parish in which the Lord's Supper is celebrated and, for the most part, *thanks* to this celebration. At least to the degree that the Church is cult-community, it actualizes itself in that moment when the eucharistic cult, in its ultimate anthropological, psychological, and sociological concreteness, is celebrated. The relationship between the total Church and the individual faith community becomes immediate. In the consideration of this relationship, justice is not factually done to the individual faith community when it is considered as "simply a part of the Church (as a governmental unit of the state)," or "when the Church is hypostatized as total Church and conceived of in a purely juridical manner as subject of the eucharistic celebration of the individual faith community" (*KuS* 76f). And he adds as consideration for further thought:

> From this point it might be possible to approach more closely the Pauline concept of the Church as total Church, and the Church as individual community in its reciprocal relationships (analogous to this would be the way that individual groups and fraternities in the time of Christ considered their relationship to the total covenant people, from which they differed and for whom they felt themselves to be representatives as mediator of its promises) (*KuS* 77).

At a time in which the phenomenon of "core communities" and the resulting possible renewal of the Church through them is increasingly a topic of discussion, Rahner's considerations for further thought take on a practical-theological relevance.[20] Here only one thought from the previous quotation will be considered, namely that the small groups of Jesus' disciples saw themselves as mediators of the promise. The Second Vatican Council took up a similar thought when it referred to the Eucharist as "the source and summit of all preaching of the Gospel" (*PO* 5/2). In this, the perspective is expanded from the purely cultic to the apostolic, the missionary, and even to the worldwide.

The Eucharist is the *source* for all the activities of the faithful that go beyond all the bounds of a narrowly conceived ecclesiality, insofar as it is the "living bread," the life-giving energy of Christ and the Holy Spirit for all. The power for evangelization through word and deed can be drawn from the Eucharist as well as nourishment for vocational work and constructive creativity. The same document from which these impulses come continues even more specifically:

> However, no Christian community is built up which does not grow from and hinge on the celebration of the Most Holy Eucharist. From this all education for community spirit must begin. This eucharistic celebration, to be full and sincere, ought to lead on the one hand to the various works of charity and mutual help, and on the other hand to missionary activity and the various forms of Christian witness (*PO* 6/5).

It could not be clearer. The *celebration* of the Lord's Supper itself has an educative and didactic function. It must furnish the participants with the greatest possible communicative ability. If it does not achieve this, if it is not the source for this, it is to be considered incomplete, insincere, possibly even hypocritical. (This is far removed from the ritualistic "conditions for validity" of the Scholastics.)

The Eucharist is the *high point* of the good news in word and deed insofar as all "ecclesial service" and "apostolic work" as well as all "human employment" stand in relationship to it; in the Eucharist, all of these together with the entire creation are offered up to God. In a similar context of thought, another text of the Council suggests that the

scope of the Lord's Supper knows no ecclesial boundaries—
neither regarding the "total" Church nor "ecclesial
groups"—within it—but reaches out to include the world of
nature: "The fruits of man's cultivation are changed into his
glorified body and blood, as a supper of brotherly fellowship
and a foretaste of the heavenly banquet" (*GS* 38/3). The
unifying and binding efficacy and finality of the Lord's
Supper, which creates the fellowship and unity of faith, is
effective for the entire universe as well. Teilhard de
Chardin's vision has apparently found an expression in
several of the Council's texts.

Beyond this, the Council's documents formulate more
the "centripetal," those components of the eucharistic
dynamic which tend toward the center. In just this sense,
even with shades of difference, the Constitution on the
Sacred Liturgy holds on to the concept of the "Church as cult
community":

> The sacred liturgy does not exhaust the entire activity of
> the Church. Before men can come to the liturgy they
> must be called to faith and to conversion.... Never-
> theless the liturgy is the summit toward which the
> activity of the Church is directed.... For the goal of
> apostolic endeavor is that all who are made sons of God
> by faith and baptism should come together to praise
> God in the midst of his Church, to take part in the
> sacrifice and to eat the Lord's Supper (*SC* 9/1; 10/1).

The power of the Eucharist to release men from their
isolation so that they can gather around a living existential
middle is then illustrated with short quotations from the
New Testament and from the Roman sacramentary:

> The liturgy, in turn, moves the faithful filled with "the
> paschal sacraments" to be "one in holiness"; it prays
> that "they hold fast in their lives to what they have
> grasped by their faith." The renewal in the Eucharist of
> the covenant between the Lord and man draws the

faithful and sets them aflame with Christ's insistent love (*SC* 10/2).

(Such descriptions make sense for the modern hearer only when the celebration of the Mass, which is described with such attracting power, becomes practical and experiential.)

The "centripetal" dynamic of the eucharistic assembly, when it is so understood, comes to expression in various ways. At one point the Council declares that it implies an invitation to all: "All men are called to this union with Christ"; the two-dimensional *communio* (*LG* 3; cf. 7/1; 11/1) is to be a truly "catholic," i.e., universal opportunity for participation. For *non-Catholic* Christians as well—indeed especially for them—is the invitation intended; even if there are still obstacles on the way to an inter-confessional celebration of the Eucharist, hope must not be lost (cf *UR* 4/3). Although the Council fathers were very probably aware of the often quite closed stance of the non-Catholic Oriental churches, they did not hesitate (and that is more than diplomacy) to regard the Oriental understanding of the Eucharist as in many respects exemplary:

> Everyone knows with what love the Eastern Christians celebrate the sacred liturgy, especially the eucharistic mystery, source of the Church's life and pledge of future glory. In this mystery the faithful, united with their bishops, have access to God the Father through the Son, the Word made flesh who suffered and was glorified, in the outpouring of the Holy Spirit. And so, made "sharers of the divine nature" (2 Pet 1:4), they enter into communion with the Most Holy Trinity. Hence, through the celebration of the Eucharist of the Lord in each of these churches, the Church of God is built up and grows in stature, and, through concelebration, their communion with one another is made manifest (*UR* 15/1).[21]

Here a practical ecclesiology of the individual, i.e., of the local church, is placed in connection with the mystery of the trinitarian communion and, at the same time, grounds are given for the collegial celebration of the ritual. In this way as well, the Lord's Supper appears as an ecclesial celebration of *communio* in and through Christ.

3.3.2.2. Christological Enabling of Community

From the total tenor of the Council's documents, the conviction becomes clear that the ecclesial unity and community which the Eucharist mediates are not possible without the singular and unique self-sacrifice of Jesus on the cross. For it is certainly not the aggregate of individuals assembled for the Lord's Supper who bring about the "two-dimensional *communio*" by their own power. This *communio* remains essentially the gift of the Giver, Christ.

Still the Council theologians show some uncertainty when it comes to the subject of designating more specifically the eucharistic act as a *sacrificial act*. There were critical voices which, in this respect, signaled a peculiar reversion of Vatican II to a pre-Tridentine stance—for example, in the case of the declaration concerning the sense of the newly rediscovered "common priesthood" of all believers where it is stated that "they offer the divine victim (*divinam victimam*) to God (*LG* 11/1; *SC* 48; *PO* 5/3). Here Christ appears to be more the passive object than the freely acting final subject of the eucharistic act. On the other hand, there are Council texts which repeat the Tridentine doctrine in all clarity: Christ "is present in the Sacrifice of the Mass not only in the person of his minister, 'the same now offering, through the ministry of priests, who formerly offered himself on the cross,' but especially in the eucharistic species" (*SC* 7/1). In this, the actual self-activity of the reconciler as subject of the eucharistic sacrifice stands out, i.e., that he is the "primary administrator" of his sacramental sacrifice. Between both poles, which are evident from these statements, are other varying declarations. In one case, it is stated that priests have "the sacred power of orders, that of offering sacrifice..." (*PO* 2/2), without clarifying the specific character of the sacrificial act. In another place it is more precisely stated that the presbyters "offer Christ's sacrifice sacramentally" (*PO* 5/1), a statement that does justice to the uniqueness of the redeeming self-sacrifice of Christ and its re-presentation through the sacramental act. Another statement has a similar content: "As often as the sacrifice of the cross by which 'Christ our Pasch is sacrificed' (1 Cor 5:7) is celebrated on the altar, the work of our redemption is carried out" (*LG* 3/1). According to this, those who "celebrate" the cross would direct their entire attention to this redeeming sacrificial act of the Redeemer, which was once accomplished for all time, as it is suggested by the "memorial" character of the Eucharist (*SC* 47). In this, the Council has reached that point which would do justice to a positive concern of the Reformers, i.e., that the participants in the Lord's Supper are commemorating Christ's sacrifice, which he actualizes really and sacramentally, and which draws the participant, by the power of this self-sacrifice of Christ, to offer himself as a real "spiritual" sacrifice. An encounter occurs (or better an "asymmetrical interaction") between the self-sacrificing Christ and the self-dedication of the individual faith—or, as the Council states: "Through the ministry of priests the spiritual sacrifice of the faithful is completed in union with the sacrifice of Christ the only mediator" (*PO* 2/4). In this sense, the sacrificial act itself already has the character of a joint act; there is a convergence and a *communio* of self-offering. Several statements emphasize that the ethical self-offering of the participant should normally always "accompany" every sacramental self-realization of Christ's sacrifice (*SC* 48; *PO* 2/4; 5/3). What Luther meant by a "spiritual sacrifice," i.e., the "sacrifice of praise and thanksgiving" by the faithful in connection with the Lord's Supper, is here to a great extent accepted.

The suspicion that such a treatment of basic Protestant concerns in the documents of Vatican II would not be

thinkable without a previous ecumenical dialogue can easily
be proven. Still, Catholic theological investigation had itself
already given sufficient impetus so that the ecclesiological
aspect of the Lord's Supper received a clearer Christological
foundation. A. Gerken summarized the results of these
investigations in his book *Theology of the Eucharist (ThEu)*
and worked them into a synthesis by his own reflections.
Only the most essential elements of these results can be
given here.

The exegetical finding—that according to the oldest
interpretation of the complex "Last Supper-crucifixion of
Jesus" (which was inspired, if not directly formulated, to an
undetermined degree by Jesus) the *personal* motive played a
larger role than the purely factual—is determinative. This
means that Jesus himself placed the accent less on the old
covenant-sacrifice, with its slaughter of the sacrificial
animals according to Exodus 24:8, as on the figure of the
servant of God who, according to Isaiah 53:10, "gives his life
as an offering for sin," freely making of himself a martyr of
Yahweh's justice (cf *ThEu* 19f, 28f). So the meaning of the
"Last Supper-cross" complex is to be found totally in the self-
sacrifice of Jesus "on behalf of many" (cf Mk 14:24; Mt
26:28).

Jesus now makes of himself, as the One who gives
himself for the many, the gift of that banquet which he
himself has desired. There occurs a self-giving of the self-
sacrificing One. The host who is willing to sacrifice himself
gives himself to his guests as the nourishment that creates
community. That area of freedom in which encounter,
exchange, unification, and integration are made possible by
his radical self-dedication to the coming of God's kingdom
on earth becomes reality in the banquet-fellowship he offers.
Therefore, his words are not directed primarily to the
material elements of bread and wine, but to eating and
drinking, i.e., to the fellowship of his invited disciples
around the table. His presence as self-giving host is meant
for them personally.[22] The offer of salvation is identified
with the person of the One making the offer, and participation occurs logically by a personal willingness of the ones

addressed to receive it. On both sides, a willingness for inter-personal encounter and communication predominates.[23] All of these considerations form, for contemporary understanding, the heart of eucharistic doctrine.

There is a double reason why it is possible to understand this complex moment of encounter, which is traceable back to the historic Jesus, as a sacramental act which can be present at any moment of time and transcends all historical distance. On the one hand, the unique mystery of Jesus in the mediation of his unique offer as host can be for all the faithful of all times a present reality when understood in the biblical sense of a "real recollection" (in Hebrew, *zikkaron*; in Greek, *anamnesis*; in Latin, *memoriale*).[24] By "real recollection" is meant something more than merely a memorial celebration, a symbolic calling-to-memory of a past event; nor is a ritual representation of a basic symbolic drama after the pattern of the mystery religions sufficient. It is to be understood more in the sense of a symbol of an ever-present and actual consciousness of the faithful. Jesus himself, according to this interpretation, meant by his statement, "Do this as a remembrance of me" (Lk 22:19; cf 1 Cor 11:24f), that the coming of the kingdom should be for all the faithful of all times accessible.

On the other hand, this becomes understandable and believable in an *eschatological* interpretation of history. Accordingly, the concisely formulated maxim of A. Gerken holds true: "The ultimate remains" (*ThEu* 57). That which historically occurred "once and for all," that which at the same time gives meaning to the past, the present, and the future, that is continually existent. It does not need to be "actualized," revived, or made present by an additional action. It unfolds its historical might of itself and at all times. The Christ-event, that Last Supper-cross-Easter complex (the resurrection in the power of the Spirit must certainly be considered as well), is actually *the eschaton* of Christian faith, God's creative, perfecting act with total historical validity. And based on its eschatological (and consequently its spirit-filled, pneumatic) character, this unique self-offer, the sacrifice, the martyrdom of Christ, remains always and everywhere effective reality.

At this point, the classical question of the "real presence" receives an *ontological* clarification. Various theologians, A. Gerken included, call on the help of M. Heidegger's existential philosophy—usually through the mediation of B. Welte[25]—in order to make this way of thinking fruitful for an understanding of the Eucharist. The point of departure here is the conception that every intellectual being can come to an understanding of himself only in his relationship to other intellectual beings. In more technical terminology, his ontological structure or nature is essentially "relational," needing and capable of inter-relationship. It is, of course, conceivable that Jesus in his desire to communicate took this human structure completely into consideration and so through his sacrifice provided an openness for the human personal sphere which is constantly and repeatedly developing. The statement of the Johannine Jesus, "The bread I will give is my flesh, for the life of the world" (Jn 6:51), would then be understood as an indication of the "relational ontology" of his person and his deed (*ThEu* 199–2107).

Regarding this ontological dimension, the early Greek Fathers had, in part, already followed this train of thought, as J. Betz has convincingly demonstrated.[26] Their thinking was, of course, "two-dimensional" according to the Platonic pattern. But they did attempt to incorporate the historical dimension of the eucharistic Christ-mystery. Accordingly, Jesus' unique saving work is a "higher" reality which ever and again comes to expression and efficacy in the "lesser" reality of the ritual act. In this way it signifies itself really. It communicates itself "real-symbolically" in the ritual mystery. This way of thinking usually does justice to that element in the Eucharist which is unalterably divine initiative and self-communication. They avoided the trend of the Hellenistic mysticism which tended to see the "higher" reality as confined and available in the ritual manipulation. Still, these older Greek Fathers did not reach either the depth of the biblical "real recollection" or the personal dimension of modern existential philosophy.

For this reason, most modern Catholic eucharistic theology tends to base the ecclesial dimension of the sacrament less on Christian versions of mystery than on philosophical concepts of interpersonal and group reciprocity. There are various attempts in this direction. One key word, however, recurs with great regularity, that of "self-representation" or "self-realization." In this way, Christ appears as the decisive author, the actual priest, the "primary administrator" of the eucharistic sacrificial act. That does not, of course, necessarily exclude the cooperation of the so-called "recipient" of the sacrament, and that the Church should be considered as a collective whole. The admonition, for example, that assuming the burden of the poverty of the poor and the weakness of the weak belongs to the essence of an appropriate celebration of the Lord's Supper is not lost from view. There are those who speak of a "mutual real presence," i.e., of the self-presentation through faith and action of the "con-celebrants" as the answer to the gracious self-presentation of Christ.[27] That includes, of course, the social commitment of the participants in the sense of Jesus' saying, "The poor have the good news preached to them" (Mt 11:5), a commitment which is referred to by various writers as a "political theology"[28] which includes an expressly social-critical mission.

All of these approaches show clearly how today the "sacrament of unity" has become a catalyst for a comprehensive rethinking of our existence as Christians and Church in the world. No other sacrament has this kind of significance.

3.4. The Sacrament of Reconciliation

In the sacrament of reconciliation, a completely different area of human experience comes into view—the *presence of evil* in world and history. The accompanying problematic of sin and guilt, i.e., of the removal of sin and of forgiveness, is reflected in all religions. A Judaeo-Christian distinction in this respect, however, is the conviction of faith that the living God *himself*, through certain interventions of his unearned mercy in the existence of groups and individuals, repels the power of evil and frees sinners from their guilt. The measure of this divine desire to forgive can only be grasped in the context of an understanding of the human need for salvation; otherwise it would be lost in infinity, in the "measurelessness" of creative-redeeming love.

In the Gospel, Jesus, similarly as in the prophetically thundering message of John the Baptist before him, proclaimed that there are essentially two conditions set for those wishing forgiveness, faith and repentance. In an *act of faith*, the individual, who is aware of his limitations, must place his entire trust in the strength of God. In the *repentance* which is motivated by this faith, he must continually strive for a radical change of his basic attitudes in that he turns from the idols of goods and interests and turns toward a life-style pleasing to God. Emerging from a conviction of faith that such an ethical renewal of one's life is possible only because of the unique saving work of Jesus Christ, the understanding of reconciliation has always demonstrated a Christ-centered perspective. Only the *ecclesial mediation* of the saving power of Christ and of God's forgiveness became from time to time the object of vehement controversy. The questioning of the sacramentality of reconciliation by the Reformation resulted in a broadly based and systematic formulation of Catholic doctrinal tradition in this respect. It was as well the task of the Council of Trent to clarify this question; and its doctrinal pronouncements were not until quite recently the objects of reconsideration leading to additions and changes in emphasis.

3.4.1. The Tridentine Teaching on the Sacrament of Reconciliation

The most pressing task for the Council of Trent was the clarification of the necessity of the sacrament of reconciliation and at the same time of its institution by Jesus Christ.

Sacramental reconciliation is *necessary* insofar as it represents the only established possibility of communicating "the benefit of Christ's death to the fallen after baptism" (*NR* 642; *DS* 1668). Baptism is indeed the fundamental mediation of the forgiveness of sins and of God's justifying grace in Christ. Still, the serious sins which disrupt the state of grace are repeated, while baptism is not. Therefore, there must be a second sacramental chance, a further ecclesial possibility to attain grace. Therefore, there exists the sacrament of reconciliation.

> The Lord instituted at that time the sacrament of reconciliation, specifically as he breathed on his apostles after the resurrection and said, "Receive the Holy Spirit. If you forgive men's sins, they are forgiven them; if you hold them bound, they are held bound" (Jn 20:22f). That by this salient act and through these clear words the apostles and their rightful successors are given the power to reconcile those faithful, who have fallen after baptism, to forgive their sins and to hold them bound, that is the concurring opinion of all the fathers (*NR* 644; *DS* 1670).

When the Council refers here only to John 20:22f as the "words of institution" (through which the sacramental institution "specifically" was supposed to have occurred), this was probably because the resurrected Lord speaks these words in the full power of the Holy Spirit; what he says is based on the already completed work of salvation. In Matthew 16:19 and 18:18, where the temporal Jesus speaks to his disciples of the binding and loosing power of "the keys of the kingdom of heaven" in the future tense, this probably meant for the Council fathers, as it did in Scholastic tradition, more specifically the promise rather than the conferral of the commission to forgive sins (cf Ott 498). Beyond this, the Council was certainly aware that the passage in Matthew—according to Calvin and other Reformers—refers exclusively to the power to proclaim the word of God, the Gospel, for the freeing of the faithful and the rejecting of the unbelievers, but refers in no way to a sacramental power of the priest to proclaim a justifying forgiveness of sins. It is noteworthy that the Council quotes Matthew 18:18 only to support its thesis of the legitimate minister of the sacrament of reconciliation. It is understandable from the standpoint of contemporary exegesis that they did not consider the question of the historicity of the words of Jesus which they quoted. The conviction gained from this account—that Jesus, who spoke in the course of his earthly existence words of forgiveness, wished to commission this group of his disciples with this same ministry until the coming of God's kingdom—could be of decisive importance.

Because Luther, who (in passing it must be noted) held to the practice of private confession to the end of his days, described reconciliation as basically only a "return to baptism," a constantly renewed memorial of baptismal grace, the Council of Trent saw itself obliged to accentuate the differences between the two sacraments. The criterion for this is found in the tradition that sacramental penance is a real and valid legal action in which the officers of the Church speak a sentence over a member of the Church who has clear knowledge of his guilt. This is not at all the case with baptism since the candidate comes from without and is subject to no prior legal authority of the Church (cf *NR* 645, 668; *DS* 1671, 1685, 1709).

The Council included as well some corrective elements regarding the *inner structure* of the sacrament. Just as the Reformation tended to a two-part determination of the (non-sacramental) penitential disposition as an act of contrition and an act of trusting faith, so it was necessary, in keeping with Catholic tradition, to emphasize the outward confession of sins and works of reparation as components of sacramental penance. A concept of this structure was derived from a synthesis of all essential traditional components. The "material" of the sacrament is the threefold disposition of the penitent: contrition, confession, and reparation; its "form" consists of the words of absolution by the priest (cf *NR* 647; *DS* 1672f).

The Council devotes remarkable space to the theme of *contrition* and in doing so strives for a biblical foundation. This goal was not reached, however, insofar as the entire range of the Old Testament concept of *"sub"* and the New Testament term *metanoia* are not sufficiently taken into consideration. The disposition for contrition appears to be much less a disposition of faith, which has God as its primary object, than of man in his moral misery. The perspective remains one-sided, centered negatively on sin. The impression here may even be of a spiritual self-flagellation when in the midst of the many negative expressions—such as "hate for sin," "holy anguish of soul," "depravity" and "death" because of guilt, "much tears and exertion," "exhausted with groaning," "bitterness of the heart," and the like—few positive expressions such as "to create for oneself a new heart and a new spirit" are not seen (cf *NR* 643, 646, 650; *DS* 1669, 1672, 1676). If it were permissible to measure these doctrinal statements against our present understanding of the biblical theory of conversion, the conciliar definition of contrition would appear to be factually incomplete and unbalanced in that it consists simply in an "anguish of the soul and an abhorrence for committed sins along with the intention not to sin in the future" (*NR* 650; *DS* 1676; cf *NR* 664; *DS* 1705). On the other hand, the division of contrition into a "perfect" and an "imperfect" form is supported by a biblically warranted notion. The former is brought into connection with that love of God which frees the human individual *from* the fascination arising out of his own feeling of guilt and *for* the broader horizons of faith. The latter is understood as produced by that wholesome fear of punishment which the wisdom of the Bible and its understanding of human nature is not afraid to present as a legitimate path to ethical improvement—even in the context of faith (cf *NR* 651; *DS* 1677f). In this way, a kind of perfectionism in the faith-life is also rejected which was not always lacking in the Protestant *"sola fide"* principle in its application to the practice of repentance.

The obligation to a complete *confession* of mortal sins—according to their kind and frequency—is understandably and rationally based on the fact that the priestly magistrate, as a representative of Christ, can make a correct judgment and is able to impose a commensurate penalty only when he has a sufficient knowledge of the circumstances (cf *NR* 652f, 655f; *DS* 1679f, 1706f). However, the Council hardly treated that more comprehensive spiritual counseling which would have given the sacrament of reconciliation a dimension and a meaning for the individual life-history as was the case in the oldest practice of Christian spirituality. Its dominating perspective remains judicial.

Its statements concerning *reparation* have a predominantly juridical context as well. The point of departure in this respect is the statement that God can indeed forgive the guilt without removing the entire punishment connected with it. Therefore, both divine justice and divine goodness, in a desire to correct the sinner, demand that the penitent receive a reparatory punishment. In this context, a solidly Christological thought appears that, at least in part, takes the Protestant "*solus Christus*" into consideration:

> In addition is the fact that, through the reparation for sins that we suffer, we become conformed to Christ Jesus, who made reparation for our sins and from whom all our ability [to do so] comes, and that through reparation we receive a sure pledge that we will be glorified with him if we suffer with him (cf Rom 8:17).

Immediately following is the doctrine of the cooperation between Christ and the just who work and live "in him," which is decisive for the entire Tridentine doctrine of justification:

> Still, the reparation that we bring for our sins is not in the sense our own, as if it were not done through Christ Jesus; for in ourselves, i.e., insofar as we are dependent upon ourselves, we can do nothing, but when he, who

strengthens us, works in us, then we can accomplish all things (cf Phil 4:13) (*NR* 658; *DS* 1690; cf *NR* 656, 671; *DS* 1689f, 1712).

And a Christocentric touch remains as well in those statements concerning *absolution*. Here the thought is expressed that the absolution spoken by the priest is "the administration of another's good deed" (*NR* 654; *DS* 1685), that is, the deed of Christ. Beyond this, however, the accent is clearly on the administration of the "power of the keys," i.e., the power of binding and loosing according to Matthew 18:18, a power given by the words of Christ to the bishops and priests (even to the wicked!), but not to all the Christian faithful without distinction (cf *NR* 653, 669; *DS* 1684, 1710). Certainly the Council wishes in this to condemn those egalitarian tendencies which, in imitation of Wycliff and Hus (cf *NR* 627f; *DS* 1260f) as well as the spiritualists of the Middle Ages, really threatened the integrity of traditional Church order. It wishes neither to hear nor to speak of any possible charismatic authorization—even of pious laymen— for the forgiveness of sins. In doing so, however, the Council excludes an entire epoch and a whole segment of Christianity—the first two centuries, during which the power of forgiving sins can hardly be proven to have been the exclusive right of bishops and priests,[29] and the Eastern half of Christianity where, at least into the thirteenth century, penance was primarily in the hands of monks who were regarded as "bearers of the Spirit." In addition, the positions of Peter Lombard and Thomas Aquinas, which held that a layman could and must make a confession of sins to another layman in the absence of a priest, is quietly passed over. And no mention is made of emergency confessions to a deacon or even of emergency absolution by a deacon which was practiced until the end of the twelfth century (cf Ott 523f).

And finally the Council sees the *efficacy* of the sacrament as largely the "reconciliation with God" which "for God-fearing people...is often followed by peace and joy of conscience with great comfort to the soul" (*NR* 649; *DS* 1674).

3.4.2. Modern Aspects
of the Theology of Penance

Similar to the case of the Eucharist, *one* particular aspect determines the direction of thought taken by the contemporary rethinking of the sacrament of reconciliation—the *ecclesial* dimension. The clear position of Vatican II is determinative for this:

> Those who approach the sacrament of penance obtain pardon from God's mercy for the offense committed against him, and are, at the same time, reconciled with the Church which they have wounded by their sins and which by charity, by example and by prayer labors for their conversion (*LG* 11/2; cf *PO* 5/1).

With this, we have the first clear statement of the teaching office concerning the idea of "peace with the faith community" (*pax cum ecclesia*) which characterized the Church's understanding of penance for centuries and leaves no trace of the rather "privatizing" statements of the Council of Trent concerning the efficacy of the sacrament. This most recent Council demonstrates in this a deeper and broader view of the subject matter. It goes into the depths in that it sees *God* clearly as the one granting reconciliation; and it widens the scope of reconciliation to include the ecclesial community which sustains the penitent and is affected by his deeds. Theologians of the Council, such as Rahner and Schillebeeckx, do not hesitate to see, in the successful dialogue between the repentant Christian and the minister of the absolution which results in the "*pax cum ecclesia*," that immediate effect of the sacramental act which results in all further effects (reconciliation with God, peace of soul). This they call the "*sacramentum et res*" of penance (cf *KuS* 84; *ChSG* 179).

It becomes clear that this new accent is a return to the sources when it is compared with the Pauline practice of penance as well as with that of the primitive Church. In his

First Letter to the Corinthians (5:1-13), Paul shows that the
exclusion of a notorious sinner who endangers the life of the
faith community is really a concern of the entire ecclesial
group. The faith community was to assemble with Paul "in
the name of our Lord Jesus Christ" and "in the Spirit"; and
"empowered by our Lord Jesus Christ" it was to pass (when
possible a "medicinal") sentence on the guilty party. And in
his Second Letter to the Corinthians, he emphasized that the
process of reconciliation is also a corporate concern in which
he, as apostle, does not necessarily need to play the
determinative role:

> The punishment already inflicted by the majority on
> such a one is enough; you should now relent and support
> him so that he may not be crushed by too great a weight
> of sorrow.... If you forgive a man anything, so do I. Any
> forgiving I have done has been for your sakes and,
> before Christ, to prevent Satan—whose guile we know
> too well—from outwitting us (2 Cor 2:6-11).

Both of these quotations from Paul show that the joint
exercise of the process of exclusion and readmittance—
apparently in the sense of the power of binding and
loosing—was an established practice in the local assembly
of the Gentile Christians already within twenty or thirty
years of Christ's crucifixion and could be employed by the
apostle at any time.

The factual situation gives a suitable context to the
words of Jesus in Matthew 18:15-19. At the end of this
passage, the well-known declaration of Jesus appears,
"Where two or three are gathered in my name, there am I in
their midst." (A number of Church Fathers interpret this as
meaning that even the smallest group of believers can be
completely the Church of Christ, since Christ desires to be
present in it.) In this context, the previous sentence promises
that the corporate prayer of the disciples, even if they are
only two, will be heard by the Father. And before this
sentence are Jesus' instructions concerning how the

community should approach a sinner in their midst—
admonishing, correcting, and finally binding and loosing.
In all of this the goal remains the "winning back" of the
sinner.

The fact that this passage was quoted only partially by
the Council of Trent (i.e., only verse 18) and exclusively as
proof of the power of bishops and priests to pronounce
absolution appears to contemporary theology as an
abridgement of its content. Without reducing the role of the
representatives of holy orders, which is meaningful,
legitimate, and necessary in Church order, contemporary
theologians hold that Matthew 18:18 cannot be separated
from its completely ecclesial context, and that the joint
responsibility of the faith community in questions of
penance cannot be lost from view. According to K. Rahner:

> These passages treat of the way in which the holy
> community of Jesus approaches a sinful member of its
> fellowship. When such a member of the community of
> salvation, which is to proclaim through its life the
> victory of grace and the coming of the kingdom of God,
> sins persistently (today we say "seriously"), it cannot be
> a matter of indifference to this Church of Jesus. (*KuS* 83)

That means, on the one hand, that the faith-community is
itself "wounded" by every "affront to God" in its midst, as is
emphasized by Vatican II. On the other hand, the same
community of faith must be active and do its part in the
process of forgiving and reconciling. A third element is
added by Rahner when he states that this desired activity of
the faith-community is self-critical, is a self-judgment of the
Church:

> What happens here in the sacrament of penance is an
> actualization of the Church's own essence. The Church
> is manifested in the penitent himself (who cooperates in
> its liturgy) as the penitent Church of sinners (*KuS* 84).

In the ancient Church, a similar consciousness of solidarity and responsibility was active. Penance was to such a degree a matter of the ecclesial community that it had to be anchored in the *Eucharist* as sacrament of fraternal *communio*. Without this relationship to the Eucharist, a genuine penitential practice was unthinkable. Not only, according to the Didache (14:1), did the eucharistic celebration begin with a public confession of sins, but the decisive punishment for sins was an exclusion from fellowship at the ritual supper. A public reconciliation of the sinner with the faith community was necessary to be readmitted to the fellowship of the Lord's table and so to enjoy reconciliation with God as well (cf Ott 500ff).

The main responsibility for penitential discipline, and therefore the power of absolution, rested by the middle of the third century in the West with the bishops and presbyters and, in case of emergency, with the deacons.[30] After introduction of private confessions, both Church discipline and theology were long uncertain of the role of the laity, i.e., of the common members of the ecclesial community, in the process of reconciliation. In fact, in the Middle Ages the Western Church never found its way back to the ecclesiality of the penitential practice in the ancient Church. The "individualism" which characterized many of the Tridentine doctrinal statements won the ascendency.

Today, the movement toward *penance services* and, under some specific circumstances, the granting of general absolution indicate a return to the sources. On the other hand, a number of theologians wish to take into consideration the achievements of modern psychology, e.g., in the form of spiritual counseling; but it must be asked if the counselors in this case really have to be priests. There is a great divergence of opinion in this area. In any case, the classical private confession is no longer seen as the only possible way to sacramental reconciliation and ethical development; and still less is the aspect of a judicial monologue in the process of reconciliation considered to be the central aspect. The key word "dialogue" takes on in this area as well a central importance; the discussion, the process of reconciliation, which develops between penitent and priest, is characterized by a cooperation, a mutually personal dialogue, a kind of "concelebration." And there are some attempts in theological discussion to consider a possible renewal of "lay confessions" with an adaptation to the modern situation.[31]

3.5.   The Anointing of the Sick

In close connection with the sacrament of penance, some things must be said about the anointing of the sick. The Council of Trent considers this sacrament in a single breath with penance as its *"consummativum,"* i.e., its special "completion" (*NR* 696; *DS* 1694). This "complementary sacrament" corresponds, according to the Council, above all to the situation of life coming to an end, in which the human individual is particularly threatened by the power of evil. Therefore it is called "extreme unction" (the last anointing).

Concerning the *sacramentality* of this ritual anointing for the seriously ill, the Council, in view of its rejection by the Reformation, wishes to leave no doubt:

> This holy anointing of the sick is truly and really instituted by Jesus Christ, our Lord, as a sacrament of the new covenant. It is indeed suggested by Mark (Mk 6:13), but it is recommended and proclaimed to the faithful by the apostle James, the brother of the Lord. He states: "Is there anyone sick among you? He should ask for the presbyters of the church. They in turn are to pray over him (another translation would be: to pray for him), anointing him with oil in the name of the Lord. This prayer uttered in faith will reclaim one who is ill, and the Lord will restore him to health. If he has committed any sins, forgiveness will be his" (Jas 5:14-15) (*NR* 697; *DS* 1695; cf *NR* 700f; *DS* 1716f).

Contemporary theologians tend to be more cautious. They are quite aware that there is no specific word of institution for this sacrament by Jesus himself and do not wish to be too quickly led by the "ritual character of the communal intercession reported by James to the assumption that a sacrament is here to be seen" (*KuS* 53; cf 52-62). At most it could be said that here is a "generic" institution of the sacrament of anointing, i.e., that the primitive Church interpreted a basic intention of Jesus (Jesus himself healed the sick) and in time recognized this as a sacrament (cf *ChSG* 121; *KuS* 56).

Concerning the *effect* of the anointing of the sick, the Council of Trent places the accent clearly on that which James places second, the forgiveness of sins. It has to do with a

> grace of the Holy Spirit, whose anointing takes away the offenses, in case there are still such to be expiated, and the remainder of sin, and strengthens and raises up the soul of the sick.

At the very end it is added that the sick "also often achieve physical recovery when it advances the salvation of the soul" (*NR* 698; *DS* 1696; cf *NR* 701; *DS* 1717).

The teaching of Vatican II is much less centered on the soul and on death—and therefore it conforms to the real sense of the passage in James. This last Council did not allow itself to be influenced by Rahner's splendid theology of death in which the anointing of the sick corresponds to the supreme moment of decision connected with it (*KuS* 61, 100f). Primarily it places physical recovery as the first goal of the sacramental intercession in that it declares:

> By the sacred anointing of the sick and the prayer of the priest, the whole Church commends those who are ill to the suffering and glorified Lord that he may raise them up and save them (Jas 5:14-16). And indeed it exhorts them to contribute to the good of the people of God by

freely uniting themselves to the passion and death of
Christ (cf Rom 8:17; Col 1:24; 2 Tim 2:11-12; 1 Pet 4:13)
(*LG* 11/2; cf *PO* 5/1).

Here as well should be noticed the ecclesial dimension of the
act; not only is the one who is sick to be supported by the
whole Church and the prayer of its priests (plural!), but he
must himself keep the common goal of the people of God in
view when he enters into the fellowship of Christ's suffering
and life.

Regarding the concrete practice of this rite, the Council
states:

> "Extreme unction," which may also and more fittingly
> be called "Anointing of the Sick," is not a sacrament for
> those only who are at the point of death. Hence, as soon
> as anyone of the faithful begins to be in danger of death
> from sickness or old age, the fitting time for him to
> receive this sacrament has certainly already arrived
> (*SC* 73).

3.6. Holy Orders

The sacrament of holy orders forms, together with
matrimony, that last group of the seven which, according to
the Scholastic concept, is essentially concerned with the
preservation of human society in its ecclesial and secular
forms of existence. Both confer equally "sacramental states
of life"; they form the total life history of those who receive
and bear them.

The sacrament of holy orders, as the cultic foundation of
the priestly and episcopal states, always became controversial among Christians when clerics were challenged because
of excessive claims to power, moral bankruptcy, or public
functional ineptitude; and the institution was then examined from the standpoint of its biblical and primitive-
ecclesial legitimacy. This occurred to a previously unheard
of extent at the time of the Reformation. The main criticisms

of the Reformers can be summarized as too little proclamation of the Word, too much sacramental "works," a widespread discrepancy between proclaimed and lived morality, and lack of a scripturally hierarchical structure, a missing clarity concerning the term "priesthood" (i.e., "*sacerdotium*"). This challenge became as well for the Council of Trent a subject needing response.

3.6.1. The Tridentine Defense of the Official Priesthood

If the Tridentine texts concerning the sacrament of holy orders are read through modern eyes, the impression may at first be given of improvisation and one-sided polemic. In contrast to the Decree on Justification and to the doctrinal statements on the Eucharist, both an earnest attempt to biblically establish its argumentation and the compactness of a systematic thinking are missing. It is no wonder that the ecumenical discussion has hardly been aided by these texts. For a correct assessment of the teaching offered here, its definitively defensive character must be considered. It wishes to offer nothing more than an apodictic defense of a very old Catholic tradition.

The first apologetic point was directed against the Protestant view that the officeholders of the Church are essentially "servants of the word" who have the sole material responsibility of proclaiming the Gospel faithfully and without deletion or addition; everything else (administration of sacraments, administrative functions) can only be understood as component parts of the correct service of God's word. In opposition to this, the Council of Trent declared that in the new covenant there is not only a "*nudum ministerium praedicandi*," a "mere service of the proclamation" of the Gospel, but as well real "priests" (*sacerdotes*) who are clothed with the *authority to offer* the "true body and blood of the Lord" and "to forgive sins" (*NR* 713; *DS* 1771; cf *NR* 715, 719; *DS* 1773, 1777). Here the term *"sacerdos"* is to be considered which, in its original definition, designated both the priest of pagan and Old Testament sacrificial ritual and the officeholders of the Christian Church—although they are never referred to as such in the New Testament Scriptures. The English word "priest," insofar as it is derived from the Greek word *presbyteros*—the "elders" of the primitive Church were referred to as such—is translated by the content of *"sacerdos"* only very imperfectly.

As a basis for this thesis the following argumentation is given:

> Sacrifice and priesthood (*sacerdotium*) are so bound to each other by divine decree that both are found in every system of salvation. Since, therefore, the Catholic Church has received in the new covenant by institution of the Lord the Holy Eucharist as a visible sacrifice, so it must also be acknowledged that there is included in this a new, visible, and external priesthood in which the old priesthood is superseded and perfected (*NR* 706; *DS* 1764).

The difference in argumentation to that of the doctrinal statements on the Sacrifice of the Mass is evident. There, the unique priesthood of Jesus Christ according to Hebrews 10:14 is referred to as the "perfection" of the Old Testament priesthood; and the characterization of the apostles and their successors as priestly servants was deduced from the unique high priesthood of the Crucified and seen as a service which caused him to be made present, to be called to memory, to be efficacious (cf *NR* 597; *DS* 1739f). For such discrepancies there is, in my opinion, only *one* more or less satisfactory explanation, that the apologetic statement on the sacrament of holy orders presupposes that the chronologically prior statement on the Sacrifice of the Mass was already well known.

After the emphatic declaration of the sacramental and sacrificial function of the *"sacerdotes"* in the new covenant, the Council states as well the *sacramentality of ordination* to the *"sacerdotium"*:

> Because it is clear according to the testimony of Scripture, the apostolic tradition, and the universal interpretation of the Fathers that through holy ordination...grace is conferred, no one may doubt that ordination is in its true and actual sense one of the seven sacraments of Holy Church (*NR* 708; *DS* 1766).

2 Timothy 1:6f. is given as the only scriptural proof as it states that Timothy had received a "gift" of grace by the imposition of the apostle's hands. Nothing is said in this respect (again as opposed to the texts on the Sacrifice of the Mass that at least mention the Last Supper command of Jesus) as to whether the imposition of hands as a grace-giving rite of ordination is traceable back to Jesus, or whether a "word of institution" by Jesus can be found. Only later in the doctrinal statements is it said that the ordination ritual is "a sacrament instituted by Christ the Lord" (*NR* 715; *DS* 1733). How this is to be understood is left to individual interpretation, which, in fact, developed the following explanation: "The institution by Christ ensues from the fact that only God, i.e., the God-man Jesus Christ, can connect causally the communication of inner grace to an outward ritual" (Ott 538; cf in contrast *KuS* 44f).

The next apologetic statement has to do with Luther's particularly radical thesis of the "universal priesthood" of all the faithful, which was based on an exegesis of 1 Peter 2:9, and was critical in reference to the clergy:

> When anyone claims that all Christians are in the same manner priests of the new covenant, or that all, without exception, are given the same spiritual authority, then this is nothing other than bringing confusion into the hierarchy of the Church which is like a "disciplined army" (Song of Songs 6:4), just as if all were apostles, all were prophets, all were evangelists, all were shepherds,

all were teachers contrary to the teaching of St. Paul (cf 1 Cor 12:29) (*NR* 710; *DS* 1767).

Against such an unscriptural leveling of all differences between the diversity of ministeries in the body of Christ, the particular "character" of the official priesthood, which is impressed upon the soul of the ordained in the rite of ordination by the communication of the Spirit, must be asserted. Because of this "character," which, just as in baptism and confirmation, is indelible, it is not possible for validly ordained priests "to become laymen again" (cf *NR* 709f, 716, 718; *DS* 1767, 1774, 1776). Scholasticism speaks in this regard of an "essential difference" between priests and laity.

Without attempting to justify the principle of "hierarchy" except from the consideration of its appropriateness (the Church should have a "well ordered structure," appear as "honorable," and awaken "respect"—cf *NR* 707; *DS* 1765), the Council sets forth the ancient tradition according to which the *bishops* "especially" (*praecipue*) belong to this "hierarchical order," are "appointed by the Holy Spirit to lead the Church of God," and are "placed over the priests" (i.e., over the simple presbyters). This concept is concretized in the fact that it is the bishops who "administer the sacrament of confirmation, ordain the servants of the Church, and have various other powers whose exercise is not allowed for those of lesser degree" (*NR* 711; *DS* 1768; cf *NR* 719; *DS* 1777).

The last point of this defense of the priesthood is directed toward the demand of Luther and Calvin that a regular election (either cooptively, by popular vote, or by co-determination of the civil authorities) for the calling and installation of Church officials should be introduced or reintroduced. The Council's answer is a decisive no; such an intervention of the laity is neither necessary nor desirable (cf *NR* 712, 719; *DS* 1769, 1777).

This is as far as the Tridentine teaching on the sacrament of holy orders goes. It can be seen how much they were affected by contemporary factors that were, at least in part, of non-sacramental nature. That, in spite of theological weakness, they were able to contribute to a real inner reform and spiritual renewal of the clergy is in all probability due to the fact that they were complemented by other factors and were placed in a more realistic context of interpretation. Many of these factors were finally formulated by the teaching office during the Second Vatican Council.

3.6.2. The Doctrine of Vatican II on Ecclesial Ministry

The new accentuation of the Catholic doctrine of the ordained priesthood, which was primarily a result of the Vatican Council II, occurred in a spirit of openness toward a number of Protestant concerns. Of course, neither a better understanding of the historical development of the Church's official structure nor the desire for reunion with the Protestant churches caused the teaching office to reject the sacramentality of ordination. Still, it broadened its perspective and included biblical elements and perspectives of the ancient Church—that were certainly not sufficiently taken into account by the Council of Trent—in its work of interpretation.

Above all, Vatican II picked up on the Christ-centeredness of the Letter to the Hebrews and acknowledged the unique "high priesthood" and "mediatorship" of Christ. The entire character of the ecclesial office (now referred to rather as ministry or *"ministerium"* than as authority or *potestas*) is placed in the context of the mission of Jesus Christ: "Christ, whom the Father hallowed and sent into the world (Jn 10:36), has, through his apostles, made their successors...sharers in his consecration and mission" (*LG* 28/1). Of course, the *bishops* appear primarily as the representatives of the one and only minister of God who share and carry on his mission. Still, the "divine right," i.e., the legitimacy of the office of ministry which has been given to priests and deacons (indeed even to all "non-official" servants of the Gospel in the world) and is based on the expressed will of Jesus, becomes evident in the light of the fundamental saving mission of Christ. On the other hand, the fulfillment of the function of these bearers of the mission is itself Christologically founded completely in the sense of the "primary administrator." It is Christ himself who through this service proclaims the word of God, administers the sacraments of faith, and directs and guides the people of God on its pilgrim journey (cf *LG* 21/1).

It is conspicuous that here and elsewhere the *proclamation of the word* is referred to as the first task of the ordained ministers of Christ, whereby all mistrust of the key Protestant term "minister of the word" seems to have disappeared (cf *LG* 11/2; 28/1; *PO* 4/1f; cf as well *KuS* 87, 92). The Tridentine equation of sacrifice and sacrificial priesthood is nowhere central, and the word, which is not a part of the sacrament, no longer appears to be the dangerous opponent to sacramental celebration.

In contrast, the traditional Tridentine division of the ministry into the three offices of bishop, priest, and deacon is basically maintained in unshortened form. (For all that, the Tridentine doctrine of the "seven ordinations" is no longer to be found.) At the summit of the "hierarchy" (the word is still used, but with less emphasis) are the bishops who, characteristically, are designated as successors of the apostles by the *gift of the Holy Spirit* and not merely by juridical succession. Factually, that is scriptural. What follows is material from the ecclesiological interpretation of the ancient Church:

> The holy synod teaches, moreover, that the fullness of the sacrament of orders is conferred by episcopal consecration.... Episcopal consecration confers, together with the office of sanctifying, the duty also of teaching and ruling (*LG* 21/2).

So the bishops act in the person of Christ, who is "teacher, shepherd and priest," and they "act as his representatives (*in eius persona*)" (*LG* 21/2; *CD* 15/1). What the term "fullness"means more specifically is not developed, but that it is mentioned demonstrates that the opinion, which since Jerome[32] has ever and again been expressed, that the episcopacy must be understood historically and theologically in the context of the presbyterate is not considered here by the teaching office. In fact, the Council sees the sacrament of holy orders realized primarily in the consecration of bishops; from here the reasonableness of the ordination to the priesthood as a sacrament is achieved by theological deduction. That this "episcopal" emphasis could for theology once and for all block a perspective for the "presbyteral" is claimed by no earnest commentator. The Council made no dogmatic decision in this respect.

> While not having the supreme degree of the pontifical office, and notwithstanding the fact that they depend on the bishops in the exercise of their own proper power, the priests are for all that associated with them by reason of their sacerdotal dignity; and in virtue of the sacrament of orders, after the image of Christ, the supreme and eternal priest (Heb 5:1-10; 7:24; 9:11-28), they are consecrated in order to preach the Gospel and shepherd the faithful as well as to celebrate divine worship as true priests of the New Testament (*LG* 28/1; cf *PO* 4/1).

The text of this Council which describes the "second degree" of the hierarchy testifies, in addition to its commendable Christ-centeredness, to a certain *unclearness* in its *view of the priesthood*. The "simple priests" are dependent in the exercise of their mission on their bishops. Further on it states in this respect that priests are "prudent cooperators of the episcopal college and its support and mouthpiece," that "they represent in a certain sense the bishop" in the local faith community, and that, as their father, they are to "obey him with all respect" (*LG* 28/2). On the other hand, they can consider themselves as "sharing in the unique office of Christ, the mediator" (*LG* 28/1) whose likeness they bear. In another text, this is stated even more clearly: Priests "are configured to Christ the priest" by virtue of "the anointing of the Holy Spirit" which signs them "with a special character" so that "they are able to act in the person of Christ the head" (*PO* 2/3; cf 12/1). As such, priests stand apart from the laity for whom no such claim to represent Christ can be made—at most they can be seen as representing the mass of the *members* of Christ's body.[33] The following picture is suggested: the priests make Christ operationally present from the side of the "head" and the laity from the side of the "members" of the body of Christ. This model is certainly not biblical. It is questionable from the purely sociological perspective, all the more so because the simple presbyteral representatives of the head are themselves seen as generally dependent upon the episcopal representatives of the same. The question must be asked as to the meaning of such a "multi-staged representation of the head."

Several practical results of the relationship between presbyteral and episcopal participants in holy orders appear less abstract and confusing, especially those which speak of the structure of the *presbyterate*, i.e., of the presbyteral assembly under the chairmanship of the respective diocesan bishop. Here the "simple priests" are seen as "indispensable helpers and advisors in the ministry and in the task of teaching, sanctifying and shepherding the people of God"; and this is made possible by "the spirit of grace and counsel," which is given by God, as well as (seen more rationally) by experience and knowledge. And this makes the demand reasonable that every bishop have a "group or senate of priests" who "represent the body of priests" (*PO* 7/12; cf *LG* 28/2). The eucharistic concelebration of the bishop with various members of the presbyterate is a sacramental concretization of collegial unity in the administration of the Church.

Concerning *deacons*, the Council states:

> At a lower level of the hierarchy are to be found deacons, who receive the imposition of hands "not unto the priesthood, but unto the ministry of service." For, strengthened by sacramental grace they are dedicated to the people of God, in conjunction with the bishop and his body of priests, in the service of the liturgy, of the Gospel and of works of charity (*LG* 29/1).

They are allowed to baptize, to distribute Holy Communion and carry it to the sick, and to minister in other similar ways. Restored as "a proper and permanent rank of the hierarchy," it can in principle "be possible to confer this diaconal order even upon married men, provided they be of more mature age" (*LG* 29/2).

The renewal which Vatican II has effected in the understanding of the sacrament of orders has not prevented further investigation. On the contrary, it has inspired it by a series of unresolved questions to even more intensive effort. At present, the following questions are particularly under discussion: an historical-critical pursuit of the understanding of ecclesial offices back to their origins in the apostolic community and to the statements of Jesus himself which indicate his intention in this respect; a semantic investigation of key theological terms such as *presbyteros, episcopos, sacerdos,* and *minister*; a fixing of the position of the priesthood within the context of a theology of the various ecclesial ministries (whereby the creation of new forms, with or without ordination, is also under discussion); a timely reflection on the "universal priesthood" and the "economy of the charismas" in the context of secular society; attempts to find a hermeneutic center for the classical threefold division of the presbyteral function into a ministry of word, sacrament, and administration; a mutual recognition of the ecclesial ministries between the various denominations; the possibility of a free choice between a celibate and married life-style.

3.7. Matrimony

If sacraments have to do with realities which touch the very core of human existence, then it is clear that the love between a man and a woman can be the subject of a sacrament, indeed can be a sacrament in itself. It can be the subject of a sign which is fraught with grace in the moment of its festive sealing in the presence of the faith-community. It can be a "lasting sacrament" in that it is given substance in the life-history of a couple in their mutual acceptance of and devotion to one another.

When, how, and under what circumstances and influences the consciousness of the sacramentality of matrimony arose in the Christian Church—i.e., in the narrower, cultic-ecclesial sense of the word—would demand a long historical explication. This much, however, can be said in the scope of this book: that the sacrament of matrimony is no more based on a specific word of institution by Jesus than are confirmation, anointing of the sick, and holy orders; and, further, that there is no clear testimony in the Christian literature of the first four centuries of the sacramentality of the marriage bond (*KuS* 39–44). And, still, the dogmatic tradition of the Catholic Church is not wrong when it speaks for its sacramentality and in doing so refers to several "indications" in the Bible which point to the conformity of the matrimonial covenant with God's will.

Here as well, the constant and changing elements of Catholic teaching will be exemplified in two segments: in its Tridentine formulation, and in the new accents of Vatican II.

3.7.1. Main Aspects of Tradition

The attitude of the Church toward matrimony can be characterized generally and basically with the following key ideas: respect for the natural drives and inclinations that cause human individuals to seek marital union; rejection of every kind of animosity toward the physical body (therefore the rejection of Waldensian spiritualism: *NR* 729; *DS* 794); refusal to regard matrimony as something purely private and profane which is removed from the responsibility of the ecclesial community of grace; concern for the freedom of the mutual consent of the partners in which the sacramental act of matrimonial union consists; a threefold designation of the goal of the marital state as offspring, loyalty, and permanence. (For the latter two points cf. Doctrinal Decree for the Armenians 1439: *NR* 730; *DS* 1327.)

These constants of tradition were questioned by Luther only insofar as he declared matrimony to be an "outward thing" which does not lie within the competence of ritual, or ecclesial legislation and jurisdiction. In close connection with this theoretical position was, on occasion, Luther's practice; he approved, for example, of the double marriage of Landgrave Philip of Hesse. The first two doctrinal statements on matrimony by the Council of Trent were directed against this theoretical and practical challenge:

> Whoever says that matrimony is not really and actually one of the seven sacraments of Gospel law which was instituted by Christ the Lord, but was invented by individuals in the Church and confers no grace, he is excluded.

The same applies to those who say that "it is allowed for a Christian to simultaneously have two wives; that it is not forbidden by divine law" (*NR* 735; *DS* 1801f; cf *NR* 734; *DS* 1800). In the eyes of the conciliar theologians of Trent, this latter opinion can only be the sign of a "false freedom of the flesh" which blinds for the absolutely clear instruction of the Bible.

That only the permanent and *indissoluble* monogamous marriage represents the will of the Creator and Savior, and that the "natural love" of the marriage partners makes them capable of grace and sanctification, ensue from three clear scriptural references. To begin with, Genesis 2:23f describes

Adam's joy concerning Eve: "This one, at last, is bone of my bones and flesh of my flesh.... This is why a man leaves his father and mother and clings to his wife, and the two of them become one body." In the second text, Matthew 19:6f, Jesus quotes a passage from Genesis and, in opposition to his enemies who insist on the Mosaic right of a man to dismiss his wife, he adds: "Let no man separate what God has joined." The Council sees in this a final clarification of the divine will concerning the matrimonial bond. The third text, Ephesians 5:25, 32, indicates the grace which makes the matrimonial bond holy and a "lasting sacrament." It is the grace which Christ earned through his willingness to suffer for humanity and which he demonstrated in his relationship to the Church, which is his bride. Here the love between a man and a woman is compared to the love between Christ and his Church, and from this comparison arises an ethical requirement: "Husbands, love your wives, as Christ loved the Church. He gave himself up for her." Because Christian marriage rests on all of these proclamations of revelation, it has a "preeminence over the matrimonial relationship of earlier times"; it is a sacrament of the new covenant (in reference to the entire scriptural evidence cf *NR* 731–734; *DS* 1797–1800).

Further, the Council dedicates several statements to the claim of the Church to have authority to set up so-called "marriage impediments" (e.g., close relationship, ordination, solemn vow of religious orders) and, in certain cases, to dispense from them (*NR* 737f, 743; *DS* 1803f, 1809). In addition, it takes a strong stand against the principle of *divorce*: "Whoever says that because of false belief, because of difficulties in mutual living, or because of the malicious absence of a marriage partner the marital bond could be loosed, he is excluded" (*NR* 739; *DS* 1805). Even adultery cannot be grounds for the divorce and remarriage of an innocent party. This is deduced not only from 1 Corinthians 7:10f, but as well from Matthew 19:6-9 which, in theological tradition, has been hotly contested. In case of necessity, only one route remains open—the "separation of bed and table" for a determined or undetermined period of time (cf *NR* 741f; *DS* 1807f).

Although not expressly considered by the Council of Trent, there are still two points to be mentioned here that have, at the same time, become permanent problems for the entire course of theological tradition: the so-called *stipulation of indecency* (or lewdness) in Matthew 5:32 and Matthew 19:9, and the so-called *Pauline privilege* of 1 Corinthians 7:12ff. In both of the Matthew passages, Jesus declares that a man "who divorces his wife—lewd conduct [literally: apart from a matter of fornication] is a separate case—forces her to commit adultery." (This could be translated: "Everyone dismissing his wife even though she has not committed fornication. . . .") In any case, after such a divorce, neither the one divorcing his wife nor the divorced wife can remarry without committing adultery. In order to preserve the *absoluteness* of Jesus' command that marriage is indissoluble (in the parallel texts Mark 10:11f and Luke 16:18, as well as in 1 Corinthians 7:10f, this is indeed the stated position), two solutions have been primarily suggested to overcome the difficulty presented by the Matthew text; it was stated that Jesus allowed a "separation of bed and table" in the case of "fornication," or instead of the translation "lewd conduct is a separate case" a more strict interpretation is given through the translation, "*even in the case of lewd conduct.*" The first solution is for the Jews to whom Jesus was speaking unthinkable; the second solution is hardly admissible philologically. When this is considered, it is understandable that a whole group of theologians (Basilius, Epiphanius, Ambrosiaster, Cajetan, Catharinus, Erasmus of Rotterdam) saw in adultery in the first place legitimate grounds for divorce and then, in the second place, for a subsequent remarriage. The theologians of the first two centuries (Hermas, Justinian, Clement of Alexandria, Origen) allow as a rule the first, but not the second (cf Ott 553f). The entire discussion cannot be considered as closed; for several theologians, the indissolubility of Christian marriage therefore contains (purely theologically) elements of relativity.[34]

The so-called *Pauline privilege* appeals to 1 Corinthians 7:12ff in order to maintain the dissolubility of a marriage between unbaptized individuals in case one of the marriage partners receives baptism and the other partner, because of this, refuses to continue living peaceably with the baptized partner. In order to protect the faith of the neophyte and—as Ambrosius teaches—to avoid an "offense to the Creator," he is freed from the first marriage bond. The exegesis of the Pauline text which supports this doctrinal theory, and the logic that attempts to connect this with genuinely basic principles of the Gospel, are, up to our own day, a matter of discussion. In any case, this presents a second relativizing moment for the law of the indissolubility of marriage.[35]

3.7.2. Contemporary Aspects

The contemporary discussion of a theology of matrimony includes, of course, the insights of the human sciences, especially of psychology and sexology. Above all, however, a basic anthropological reflection, which differs materially from that of the classical period and the Middle Ages, seeks to better understand the essence of marital love in its Christian form of expression.

Nothing could serve to demonstrate this better than the words of the Pastoral Constitution on the Church in the Modern World ("Gaudium et spes") of Vatican II:

> The intimate partnership of life and love which constitutes the married state has been established by the Creator and endowed by him with its own proper laws; it is rooted in the contract of its partners, that is, in their irrevocable personal consent. It is an institution confirmed by the divine law and receiving its stability, even in the eyes of society, from the human act by which

the partners mutually surrender themselves to each other; for the good of the partners, of the children, and of society this sacred bond no longer depends on human decision alone. For God himself is the author of marriage and has endowed it with various benefits and with various ends in view (*GS* 48/1).

It becomes evident in the examination of this text as well as its continuation that it is less important in this theology than it was in the past to establish a strict hierarchy of "goods" or "purposes" for matrimony. It is no longer stated as it was in earlier theological handbooks:

The primary objective of matrimony is the procreation and rearing of children. The secondary objective is mutual assistance and the morally ordered gratification of the sexual drive (Ott 552; according to the decree of the Holy Office "De finibus matrimonii," 1944; *DS* 3838).

Neither is it any longer suggested that the secondary objectives are to be essentially subordinated to the primary. The Council is more concerned that all of the natural aspects of matrimonial love are seen in their concrete and existential correlation, whereby the central aspect is the *mutual sharing* of the partners. The terms that are used in connection with the adjective "mutual" are indicative: "surrender," "self-giving," "fidelity," "help," "affection." The reciprocity in this living community of marriage, which is so expressed, extends to every component, from sexual intercourse[36] to prayer.

It remains a prime fact that this "hermeneutic middle" of the marital state, which is far beyond the ability of the partners themselves, is enabled by the power of *Christ*. The sacrament signifies the love of Christ for mankind and takes part in it (*LG* 11/2). And just as the love of Christ is made concrete in his willingness to give himself for others, in his sacrifice for the people of the new covenant, so matrimonial love is to be an uninterrupted "for-each-other" to the point of mutual self-sacrifice. It must be observed that "Gaudium et spes" does quote Ephesians 5:25 in this context, but it has the courage not to follow Paul's analogy completely; not only the man is likened to the self-sacrificing Christ.

The reciprocity of the married couple, which is in this way Christologically substantiated, is then used as a support for what was earlier described as "natural law" or "divine order": "The intimate union of marriage, as a mutual giving of two persons, and the good of the children demand total fidelity from the spouses and require an unbreakable unity between them" (*GS* 48/1). To what extent this kind of positive argumentation concerning the unifying strength of marriage remains just a nice theory, and to what extent marriages that fail (e.g., in the sense of the breakdown of a marriage) must be taken into account, are questions still open to discussion.

The *procreation* of children appears as well *within* this correlative context and is no longer an abstract and patriarchal-dynastic glossed-over "primary objective" of the marriage contract; it is the climax, the unfolding, the fruit, the freely accepted creative result of a responsible union of love. That does not prevent a childless marriage from being in the sacramental sense a "complete community of life," for—as it is specially stated—"marriage is not merely for the procreation of children" (*GS* 50/3). Where, in the normal case, children are present, they are the special objects of the more than pedagogical affection of the parents who, through the "charism" of the marital state, have a truly apostolic mission. Indeed, Christian families are to be "what might be regarded as the domestic church" in which "the parents, by word and example, are the first heralds of the faith with regard to their children" (*LG* 11/2; cf *AA* 11). So, the matrimonial state is a thoroughly "apostolic" state in which fundamental apostolicity (in addition to unity, sanctity, and Catholicity) is translated inwardly as well as (obviously) outwardly into reality. The believing couple, with their mutual fellowship in Christ, may be considered—as Rahner writes—"the smallest, but veritable cell of the Church" (*KuS* 99). Even more so is the family with children a real appearance of the one, apostolic Church of God by reason of this sacrament of matrimony come to its consummation.

Chapter Four

TOWARD A COMMUNICATIONS THEORY OF SACRAMENTS

The history of Catholic teaching on sacraments cannot conceal its many variations. Each sacrament has its very own specific "personality"; it cannot be defined uniformly and clearly with finality, or be reduced to an *a priori* schema. It transcends, under the pressure of the times, the guidelines defining its practice and theory. If the attempt is to be made, in spite of all variations, to establish and make understandable a "unity" of sacraments—and this is certainly unavoidable for a right understanding of them—then, in the midst of the most faithfully preserved traditions, a new dimension of variability must be considered.

To begin with, the New Testament concept of *mysterion*, and then the old Roman concept of *sacramentum*, demanded the attention of those attempting to systematize. Soon after came neo-Platonism—both with and without the influence of the mystery religions. This original-copy system gave Augustine the material for his theory of symbols in which the sacramental became a two-dimensional complex of symbol and matter. Then the Aristotelian dialectic of cause and effect again offered something new; what was seen as a system of symbols now became further illuminated as a dynamic hierarchy of secondary causes deriving from the divine Prime Cause. The Lutheran restoration of a theology of the word as the primary basis for the sacramental could not successfully assert itself with the Tridentine fathers. Not until Casel's rediscovery of the old "cult mystery" did new blood flow through Scholastic arteries. But still, in an era of secularism, this attempt at a cult-centered mystery-theology could not effect a permanent victory. Karl Rahner's ontological description of being as a self-revealing, speaking, manifesting Being, and Schillebeeckx's personalistic approach, which speaks of the encounter between God and man, apparently have stronger appeal for the modern generation.

That great systematic endeavor deserves special mention which designates all sacraments as "self-expression of the Church" through the concept of the "Church as original sacrament." Even Vatican II gave guarded approval to this concept, at least insofar as it designates the people of God several times as the "sacrament of saving unity" in the service of the encounter with God and the unity of mankind (*LG* 1/1; 9/3; 48/2; 59/1; *AG* 5/1; *GS* 42/3; 45/2; cf *DV* 2). Still, the final clarification of this synthesis (or collective?) of deutero-Pauline, Augustinian, and existential philosophical elements has not yet been achieved, and practical theology is still asking the question as to how this might be possible. The fact that "sacramentality" is so variously expressed (in the context of such experiential realities as Jesus the Christ, the Church and the ritual of the Church), and that the basic concept of sacrament is so ambiguous (lying somewhere halfway between the deutero-Pauline *mysterion* and the Augustinian *signum*), causes more confusion than satisfactory understanding among theologically interested people of our time.

4.1. A Theoretical Approach

The question can be asked as to whether the last word about the sacramental in the sacraments has already been spoken so that the one "introducing" this heretofore so "dynamically changing" doctrine need only quote what has already been said. Or does he have the freedom to search for a new synthesis—after consulting people living in our modern industrial society—which includes elements previously considered in a less than systematic fashion? Is it not his responsibility to outline a working hypothesis which can perhaps contribute—in a scholarly willingness for self-revision—to a better understanding of the individual sacraments in the context of modern *experience and practice?*

The legitimacy of such an undertaking is, in my opinion, in part established by the method employed by the last Council. They apparently had two intentions: (a) to avoid definitions that give the impression of being final (even the essence of the Church was only "described"), and (b) to attempt to identify relevant truths for modern Christianity that have a primarily practical theological perspective. In fact, the Council began with the *liturgy*, to which its very first document, *Sacrosanctum Concilium (SC)* was dedicated. Here the sacraments appear, not only in the context of worship according to the (mystery) model of the primitive Church, but in the context of a consideration of factors presented to us by the research of the modern sciences of communication and the humanities. Sacraments, liturgy, and their context in the life of the world have essentially to do with a correlation between "speech and action," i.e., between "doing and speaking." The "active participation" of those "concelebrating" (those who are also participants in the everyday actions which are illuminated by faith) is emphasized (*SC* 11; 21/2; 27/1; 48; 50/1) as is the understandable and conscious communication (above all in the native language) within the concrete faith-community (*SC* 34; 36; 54/3; 72). So the Church appears as *communicative community* in its very *essence*. For it is the saving community of the speaking and acting God (cf *SC* 33) to whose basic constitution belong "maxims" which not only instruct, but also move the emotions (cf *SC* 33/3). This basic constitution is incarnated in the one intercessor and "medium," Jesus Christ, with an *eschatological finality*, so that he has become in all times and cultures the mysteriously present main speaker of the community's work and the main doer of the community's deeds (*SC* 7/1; cf *LG* 21/1). He is the head who constantly communicates with his members (*SC* 7/3; 10/1) and encourages them and enables them to communicative interaction.

These few intimations are sufficient to indicate in what sense and with which reservations the Council's method of thinking encourages a new reflection on the sacramental and on the sacraments from a communications-theoretical perspective—but certainly not merely in a technical sense which is only concerned with the empirical "how" of the word-and-deed-event. It would be profoundly insufficient and theologically questionable if a mere description of functions were offered for the processes in the "open system" of sacrament and community. An approach employing communications theory for a theology of sacraments can appeal to the Council only when, in addition to the necessary communications processes (informing, teaching, learning, challenging, making room), the area of existence and being is taken into consideration. Certainly modern communications theory has of its own no particular existential or especially ontological interest. Still, in its theological application it must be "enriched" with the elements presented by the fundamental depths of human existence, much as the Aristotelian philosophy of causality, which Thomas Aquinas borrowed, was adapted to the unspeakable mystery of grace. For only from these depths can we adequately speak of the definitive encounter in the individual life-history between grace and faith. The borrowing of thought categories or even methodology from the human sciences is allowable only under the condition that they can be expanded to include a concrete ontology of the person in his subjective and social contexts of existence. Seen from a Christian understanding of *God's* being, nothing would prevent such borrowing. On the contrary,

God's being itself includes communicative structure; he is essentially "word" and deed, binding and communicating himself; he stands in *reciprocal relation* to himself.

Based on these last statements, it can be asserted that the "substance" of the sacrament, the reality which is ultimately its content, God in his "gracious" openness to man, has a thoroughly communicative nature. The same is also true for the aspect of "sign" or "symbol" since that which points out should be at the same level as that being pointed to. Because the fundamental reality of all sacraments is God in his tendered self-communication, his effective presence serves in an *appropriate* way only that word which is capable of communication and only that deed which has a (giving-receiving) reciprocal character. The question concerns just such an appropriateness between grace in person and its "mediation" with regard to the actively receiving addressee.

Of course, seen from God's perspective, words and deeds that are estranged from or even contrary to such communication (e.g., apathetically muttered words of consecration, or a fulfilling of the "obligation" of matrimonial love out of mere habit) do not necessarily rob the divine self-communication of all its power. Still, such exceptional instances of the "persistent" love of God, which is completely undiscernible and immeasurable in its specific expression, dare not be codified, and much less become the central object of theological reflection. And this is all the more so since God, in the first place, communicates his grace not alone through the sacraments and, in the second place, has the absolute freedom to make decisive allowances for human rejection and apathy. Instead of speculating about borderline cases, it would be good to place "goal-oriented standards" of sacramental celebration in the foreground and add to the dogmatic teaching an *ethic* of a sacramental economy of exchange. That which is demanded by such an ethic, that which *should* occur, is nothing other than that a promising inter-personal process of communication allows itself to be taken into the service of God's desire to communicate himself; or, from an Augustinian perspective, that the "symbol" participate in some real way in the dynamic of the "object" it symbolizes.

To trace this approach back to its biblical roots, there are a number of possibilities that offer themselves which, however, can be treated here only in an exemplary and brief manner: the Creator who desires to have his image in the creative human individual; the love of Christ for friend and foe which continually demonstrates and expresses itself in love of neighbor; the Christ-community of the Lord's Supper which finds its symbolic expression in the Christians' mutual acceptance of each other; the discipleship of Jesus' followers who *shape* his words and *live* his deeds in an exemplary fashion. Certainly such modes of behavior are, biblically, seen more in the context of the person than in the context of objects; and, therefore, they are designated by such terms as "testimony" and "service," rather than by such words as "sign," "symbol," or "sacrament." Still, the *a fortiori* argument is here valid—that if the goal-oriented standard of the relationship between God and his faithful is referred to as a "conforming" or a "following," then the demand is all the more valid that there should be the highest possible priority established for the values which regulate the objective function of mediation between God and human individuals.

4.2. The Locating of the Sacraments

All previous analyses of the sacramental economy of salvation had as their point of departure a composite picture of God, Christ, the Church, and the sacraments. These "components" were used as well for a detailed structural analysis. Today the human individual, in his personal and inter-personal reality, has, as never before, been added to this picture. From the vantage point of the human sciences, the human individual constitutes the point at which all sacramental theological reflection begins. Notwithstanding the already mentioned claim that the *divine* attitude of communication is basis and norm for the corresponding human sphere, and not the reverse, the human individual is considered in his fundamental and concrete autonomy and *so* made the addressee of the divine norm. That means that a contemporary theology of sacraments consciously *does not begin* with the consideration of the individual as caught up in a process of becoming divine, becoming Christian, becoming a member of the Church or a communicant of sacraments. It begins with the level of his anthropological character and his common modes of behavior. The theological analysis, therefore, is preceded by a philosophical-anthropological, psychological, or sociological analysis and is further complemented by the perspectives of the behavioral sciences and cultural theory. The method is accordingly more inductive and less deductive, as it was in Scholasticism. Above all, this investigation seeks to determine which possibilities, abilities and openness are to be found in the human individual, and which concrete chances are offered in this respect by his social-psychological and cultural circumstances. Then the individual, who has been considered from these perspectives, is, in a second step which remains absolutely determinative, confronted with the demands of the sacramental ethic and with the promises of the corresponding doctrine of grace. In this way, that "correlation" remains always in view that simultaneously from without and from within conditions the active and passive aspects of the "recipient" of sacraments.

(a) Philosophical *anthropology*, summarily seen, paints a picture of man in industrial society which, in general, accentuates the encounter-theories of Schillebeeckx. Here the individual appears as an *intellectual* being in contrast to all other beings. He possesses a spirituality and brings with him his own personal mystery to which he can give a degree of access only by his *free* self-communication. The human spirit makes itself known. It reveals and imparts itself. And it does so through its own *corporality*; its words are organically articulated and disclosed, and its deeds are formed through meaningful gesture and mimic. The human individual as an intellectual being "relates" himself physically and so offers himself for an *encounter* with other intellectual beings, with fellow human beings and with God. Of course, such physically effected intellectuality does not result in every instance in a successful "revelation" of one's self—of the inner, personal, mysterious, and therefore, for others, challenging core of the personality. Much in this process of physical communication is more of a hindrance than a help for self-revelation and encounter. A *veiling* remains always a part of the process of unveiling. This need not be understood as something *negative*, as failure, weakness, or inhibition. It is just because the individual never presents himself to the surrounding world and its clutch as a totally open book that his personal mystery is never completely solved and is never completely reduced to the level of objective availability. There remains for the individual and for his freedom a vitally necessary vestige of mystery, so that the individual is able, through word, gesture, and deed, to bring ever *new* aspects of this inner treasure to communicative expression. He always has symbols available that express himself in ways not previously revealed (cf *ChSG* 9f).

It is a shame that Schillebeeckx applies this personalistic approach all too quickly to God in his appearance as incarnate revelation in order to formulate the divine economy of sacraments in Christ with modern terminology. Indeed, it has always been considered legitimate to use this person-analogy in describing God, particularly in respect to the divinity of the man Jesus. And still more so today, as the so-called "negative theology" experiences a renaissance, a theology which describes God as being "completely other," as being undescribable, we have no other choice. And especially in the area of sacramental teaching, before any application of the theological person-analogy, the anthropological person-analysis should be considered. Only in this way can it be soundly established to what degree the "communicant" himself, in his personal existence, is called by grace to a sacramental cooperation.

One possibility to determine how the human individual can be sacramentally active in our modern socio-cultural context (which implies much more than merely receiving sacraments) is offered by modern communication's theory. This helps us to understand that the individual is not viewed as isolated or dependent upon himself in his own freedom, but as participating in the interwoven context of systems which are *a priori givens*. Language, ritual, gestures, even various reflexes of thinking, feeling, and acting are not creatively invented or devised in every situation by the subject of communication. The total Catholic system of sacraments and the individual sacraments as component systems present objective demands that the subject must freely accept or reject. The fact, which is also undisputed, that this acceptance or rejection possesses *creativity*—or should possess it—does not contradict the fact that the total system is an *a priori given*. It forms rather a correlative dialectic unity.

A further contribution of communications theory to the understanding of the sacramental activity of man is found, in my opinion, in the principle of *interaction*, which will be discussed in more detail later. Here it needs only to be mentioned that the human individual is not only the sovereign producer of language, actions, revelation, and concealment (as an abridged form of personalism might suggest), but a communicator and communicant who is necessarily oriented toward reaction, reciprocation, reception and non-reception. He stands most certainly in the presence of others as the one speaking of himself, giving of himself, revealing himself. And, still, he cannot simply make his surroundings into an auditorium for his self-communication or into an arena for his physical self-expression. These surroundings themselves give answer and react. They impose upon the communicating subject their own information and counter-information so that between both parties, between the individual and the collective, an always relevant dynamic component system is created which exerts a *controlling* influence over the behavior of *both* participants. And this is the way that sacramental celebrations should develop: they should all have con-celebration character. It certainly would not do injustice to the biblically attested original intention of baptism and the Lord's Supper when it is principally stated that all of those participating in the celebration are called to *simultaneously* be receivers and senders, communicants and communicators. The individual who either only consumes sacraments or seeks to exert arbitrary control over them is neither a true communicant nor a Christian in the biblical sense. In the midst of the cultic celebration, the faithful must furnish evidence of his character as *animal interactivuum* and in this way participate in the dialogue of grace offered by Christ.

(b) The basic intention of Catholic sacramental teaching would certainly be misconstrued if the *Christological* dimension of sacramental communication were lost to view. To prevent the liturgy of the effective signs of grace from sinking into a bleak and falsely understood one-dimension exercise of group dynamics, it can be adequately celebrated only in the awareness that the dynamic of exchange, which is concretely performed and empirically grasped, is rooted *by faith* in the fundamental reality of the eternally relevant Jesus Christ. It is not even necessary to here employ the analogy of the person-concept in order to speak of a real self-revelation of the creative, redeeming God. The entire historical reality of Jesus of Nazareth, especially his self-identification with the faithful who are called to repentance, and his hospitality toward both the just and sinners, cannot be ineffectually and only *pro forma* called to memory. Because this humanity of Jesus made his unique *oneness with God* concrete and anticipated his powerful existence-for-mankind even unto death and beyond into the realm of life, the sacramental *memoria* of these facts bear in themselves the power of saving rebirth.

Paul himself stated that the crucified and resurrected One was and is in person the *mysterion* of God. This, of course, referred to the supra-cultic reality of the Jesus Christ who offered his life and death to God. Contemporary discussion of Christ as the "originally sacramental word" of God or simply as the "original sacrament" approaches, in my opinion, all too near to the cultic in order to adequately establish the cult itself. The danger cannot be completely avoided that the glorified Christ be falsely stylized according to the model of a rite, an objective cultic celebration, or a mystically glossed-over quantity. Those medieval theologians who only considered the sacramentally measurable "benefits" of the Blood of Christ which "washes away all sins" indeed fell prey to this danger and so made his total human and historical reality into something material and concrete. And it is questionable whether a modern mystery-theology with its discussion of the "Easter mystery" which is made present by the ritual has always been able to avoid this objective danger.

A communications-theoretical approach to sacramental Christology could, in my opinion, contribute to maintaining complete respect for the person and the uniquely personal mystery of Jesus in his glorified existence as the Christ. This can best be done by taking seriously his designation as "mediator" (devoid, of course, of its Platonic sense) in the later texts of the New Testament (cf 1 Tim 2:5; Heb 8:6; 9:15; 12:24). Behind this term is, of course, a rich complex of Old Testament symbolism, and rabbinic and Hellenistic tradition which cannot be analyzed here.[1] The prevailing thought seems to be that Jesus is the *new Moses*, the prophetic "co-worker" with God in the realization of his new covenant with its eschatological power and universal scope, who is therefore also the unique and final spokesman, intercessor, and high priest of mankind. The motive of the *servant of God* may as well play a not unimportant role in that Jesus was understood not merely as a mediator of information or of ritual, but as *the* mediator who gave his life for the thing mediated and therefore received God's unheard of gift of resurrection from the dead. Or stated in a more contemporary way, he is the one who committed himself totally to the overcoming of that great breakdown in communications between man and God, i.e., the "sins of the world."

What is meant by all of this transcends by far the character of a mere occurrence, object, or symbol as it is understood in a *mysterion* of God. These could only contain the idea of interaction in an analogous or expressly personalized sense, while the term "mediator" *in itself* indicates a personal and active *ministry of communication.*

The bearer of such a functional title certainly unites in himself all the poles of a communications system: sender, receiver, medium. He sends, receives, and mediates all in one, and this on the part of God as well as on the part of man. Therefore it can only be seen as just and reasonable when Jesus Christ, who is so understood (before any thought of his "two natures"), is conceived of as the source, enabler, and primary author of all sacramental communication in the new covenant.

(c) The position or place of such communications, which is *the Church* as community of Christ, is easily determined. According to our chosen approach, the Church is no longer seen as possessing an indeterminate universal "sacramentality" which could be, in certain circumstances, misunderstood as having an *ex opere operato* efficacy. The thought, which in any case is utopian, that the Church could be an effective sign of grace by very fact of its existence is totally discarded. In contrast to this, the biblically attested idea of smaller and larger groups of communicatively capable *witnesses* of the proclaimed and lived Gospel becomes central. And when the required basic attitude of these ecclesial groups must of necessity be universally characterized, then the term "ministeriality" (i.e., a fundamental ability and willingness to serve) would be appropriate. The Church, insofar as it is the Church of Christ, is God's communications-collective among men, often existing in a state of inner and outer contradiction, but always the sending-receiving *ministra Dei.*

Understandably, it is more difficult to assert this for the

universal Church than for a local community. How the world Church, in its reality that today is seen almost completely statically, can appear as universal community is at the most dependent upon ecumenical councils and other such mass assemblies. Nevertheless, Vatican II wanted to give the ancient Church practice of *communio ecclesiarum* new validity on a universal plane. This consists in a responsible exchange and fraternal sharing of goods among the various regional and national churches, the rich as well as the poor, and this by virtue of the principle of "catholicity" (cf *LG* 13, 23, *passim*).[2] Such mutual caring of all faith-communities for one another is founded characteristically, on the one hand, on the work of God's Spirit and, on the other hand, on institutions with universal scope (councils, international commissions in Rome, synods, Caritas International, information centers, etc.).

In spite of this, the concrete *local church*—beginning with the "domestic church" (*LG* 11/2) which is the family, extending to fraternities of priests living and working in community and having in some cases a community of goods (*LG* 28/3), and extending further to the local church where the pastor (or for the diocese the bishop) bears the responsibility for the *communio*—is the actual embodiment of the principle of the mutual "ministeriality" of service. These are all concretely experiential communicative component systems, systems that Paul had in mind when he presented his charismatic theory of community to the Corinthians and Romans. Certainly all the constructive reciprocity of gifts and ministries in this charismatic ecclesiology of the local church (whose locality is not to be seen primarily in a geographical sense)[3] is based on the free and unplannable working of the Holy Spirit. And, still, the success of this economy of exchange includes real empirical and observable (and in part *institutionally* determined) elements and moments that are shaped by human knowledge and ability.

In this way, the cultic institution of sacraments in the local church appears as an organic part of its communications dynamic. Whether it is the sacraments of initiation through which the youth or the adult catechumen is introduced to the language of faith-dialogue in the traditional credo-code of the community; whether it is the eucharistic celebration in which the community members, in spite of their otherwise lacking togetherness, experience themselves as communion partners through their believing participation in the unique meal of Christ; whether it is that moment of discussion in the context of reconciliation in which strength and light for a new moral beginning is mediated by the mutual self-revelation of penitent and priest; whether it is the concelebration of several priests at an ordination or the marriage of two communicant lovers in which friendly intercessory prayers give encouragement: all of this—in part institutionally and in part with charismatic creativity, at times with words and symbols, at times with contemplative silence—makes the essence of the community of Christ, as a communicative community of service, concrete reality. It makes the act of exchange tangible which arises from the soil of "mutual ministeriality" (or more traditionally of the "mutual priesthood").

The basic fraternal-collegial structure of the Church of God, which was also rediscovered by Vatican II, is another element which must be considered. The Council did indeed have the courage to open the door to the horizontal structure of "concentric" collegiality and solidarity as it was understood by the ancient Church in addition to recognizing the vertical structure of the hierarchy as it was conceived in the Middle Ages. That, in part, has become the cross of the post-conciliar period. In any case, however, this "opening" to an official and unofficial cooperative ministry—in the sense of coordination instead of a simple subordination—has given rise to a well-founded hope that our faith-communities will in the future become areas of increasingly free interactive communication in which informative feedback from all areas of the community—in the sense of a "mutual obedience"—will give rise to a dynamic control of the entire "system." The principles of collegiality and fraternity also determine anew the place and function of the sacraments.

(d) The location of the sacraments should have gained a very specific determination from these anthropological, Christological, and ecclesiological considerations. Seeing that man is essentially *animal communicans* (it is impossible for him not to "set forth," not to "transmit"), it becomes evident that Jesus Christ is the revealed mystery of God as Creator of a comprehensive communicative history in which the Church of Christ has its meaning as both a "local" and a "universal" communications entity. To the constituting activities of this entity belong, among other things, the sacramental acts of the concrete community, whose multiplicity is difficult to systematize but demonstrates nonetheless the rich aspects of the Christian life as being totally human.

Before the communicative character of the sacraments is analyzed more thoroughly, a (hypothetical) definition may be helpful. The sacraments can be understood as *systems of verbal and non-verbal communication through which those individuals who are called to Christian faith enter into the communicative process of the ever concrete faith-community, participate in it, and in this way, borne up by the self-communication of God in Christ, progress on the path of personal development.* According to this definition, the sacraments of Christian ritual would not be simply "self-realizations" of a mystical Church which is empirically difficult to grasp, but they would be events of encounter between grace and the faith of individual members of a concrete faith-community in their personal and particularly oriented individuality.

4.3. The Structure of the Sacraments

With the reservation that every sacrament has its own historical development and, therefore, its very own unmistakable structure, our theoretical approach still allows for a common structural foundation for all the factually existing sacraments. In this respect, the situation has not essentially changed regarding our understanding of sacraments since Augustine; the basic concept of "sign" used in his conceptual theory remains as before the probable, indeed in certain circumstances even the necessary generic term and common denominator. Accepted that the Augustinian "symbol-theory" can be seen in one respect as the anticipation of contemporary information- and communication-theory, it is obvious that in a resulting structural analysis of the sacraments, Augustine's twofold division of *signum et res*, of symbol and symbolized reality, will be maintained, without, of course, accepting the Platonic dualism-of-being associated with it.

4.3.1. The "Symbol"

When it is said that sacraments are *systems* of verbal and non-verbal communication, the danger is avoided of thinking of isolated words or signals. Indeed, this means that a sacrament is the part of a whole structure of communication which consists of many components.

4.3.1.1. Speech

The extent of the linguistic complexity of sacramental "symbols" will be made clear in the six following observations.

(a) A sacrament can be understood as a linguistic structure in which not only verbal speech occurs, but also non-verbal information. The *verbal* component, with its concepts, sentences, and clarifications, corresponds to all that can be *thought of* as the "mystery" that is to be revealed, both of man and of God. It functions as well as a factor which determines, distinguishes, and organizes. It is not by chance that among the words that are spoken in a sacramental celebration, most of them, ritualized by liturgical tradition, provide a firm foundation for identifying and interpreting the particular sacrament as a rite of the Christian or Catholic Church. The *non-verbal* component corresponds to all that can be *suggested* and therefore communicated *only* through images and symbols in the occurring event of encounter between the various mysteries. A whole list of means of communication serves this purpose: sound-signals, silence, eye contact or physical contact, posture, gesture, mime, symbolic pictures, colors, locations, clothing, rhythmic movement, etc.

In such communication forms, the thing signified literally becomes "corporeal," and that in a more synthetic manner than through purely verbal expression. Usually more is "communicated" more directly than through words alone. For, on the one hand, the unspeakable moments of the event are brought together and, on the other hand, the sense organs of the "concelebrating" participants are simultaneously addressed.[4] It is therefore possible that the needs of children and uneducated adults are more than adequately satisfied. The non-verbal component of sacramental celebration forms, of course, an area in which that self-communication of those celebrating, which is not fixed by the laws of ritual tradition, can develop relatively freely.

It would be incorrect at this point to favor the non-verbal over the verbal. It is necessary to strive for a *reciprocity* and a *balance* between the two. Too little of the non-verbal component would place the sacrament in danger of becoming too abstract; too little of the verbal component would surrender it to the power of regression, confusion, and—as was the great plague of the pre-Reformation era—of a magical obscurantism. In fact, word and gesture form a *correlative unity* which must be maintained in the midst of the many legitimate developments of sacramental practice and piety. Vatican II showed itself to be well aware of this fact (cf e.g. *SC* 30; 35/2).

(b) Second, the sacramental "symbol" structures itself as simultaneously an *open* system and one *handed down* by tradition. It consists, on the one hand, of a code which has been developed by the Church through long years of practice and reflection into a common medium of communication. The sacramental code is an historical development and, as such, bears its own particular normative character. This includes the advantage that it is in principle able to unify individuals, who are socially and culturally very dissimilar, in an intelligible, "catholic" celebration. If it were not for this common code, very possibly a communication with universal dimension would not be possible.

On the other hand, this handed-down language of the sacraments dare not be considered as a fully closed system. It is not a completely perfected tool for the communication of word and grace, but it is in this respect a creative instrument. The concelebrants, the "senders" and the "receivers," have the freedom to contribute in this context those relevant elements which need addressing. They are permitted—*sit venia verbo*—to ride the gift-horse creatively. They are motivated to do this by the very laws of human communication as schematized in the following three statements: (1) every human individual codifies like *all* other human individuals (i.e., according to universal norms); (2) every human individual codifies like *some* other human individuals (i.e., according to the customs of his group); (3) every human individual codifies like no other human individual (i.e., spontaneously improvising according to his own personal and immediate inspiration).[5] If, then, these three moments more or less control every occurrence of communication, all the more so must they not only be allowed in the liturgy of Christian sacraments, but they must be consciously sought, especially since it is a matter lastly of the free working of the *Spirit of God* in the midst of ritual.

And so, as a structural component of sacramental language, a second *reciprocal relationship* with its own demand for balance can be added: continuity and originality, that which remains and that which is unparalleled, diffuseness (redundancy) of time-honored linguistic figures and flashes of original expressions of faith, repetition of ritual formulas (which often has a calming and "sheltering" effect) and spontaneous outbreak of that which is experienced here and now (which could possibly have a wholesomely disturbing effect in the ritual community).[6] Unfortunately Vatican II expressed no particularly encouraging word for such freedom in celebration (cf *SC* 23/1). A rampant liturgical anarchy in many places conceivably led to a suppression of the concept of creativity or spontaneity in relation to the sacraments. Still, everyone aware of the constructive impact of the various small faith-communities will be less fearful that the balance in favor of tradition will be broken in the long run.

(c) Third, a correlation can be shown in the fundamental structure of the sacraments between both moments which are designated by the technical terms "analogical" and "digital" communication. "Analogical" refers to those communications which are charged with affect and address the affective, thereby maximally employing pictures, symbols, rituals, and gestures, creating and strengthening in this way the bonds within a particular group. A living *celebration* of the sacraments which is in harmony with the sensibilities of the participants fulfills these conditions. "Digital" (taken from the term *digit* or number) refers, on the other hand, to those moments of communication which include conceptual, logical, and sometimes argumentative perceptions which verbalize and clarify facts so that the listeners are able to make cognitive progress and are aided in decision-making. Here "information" occurs in the sense of the word as understood in our technological civilization; normally, however, a commitment is not demanded by digital communication. In this category, for example, would be the homily which accompanies the sacramental celebration and attempts to explain its meaning theologically in the context of faith experiencing the mystery.

Here, as well, certain extremes must be avoided: "A purely analogically communicating faith would be, in extreme cases, devotionalism; its digital opposite would result in a dogmatizing orthodoxy" (Bastian 69). All reformers of the substance of Christian sacramental celebration knew and know this. Calvin, for example, advocated strongly that baptism and the Lord's Supper were to be understood as real moments of proclamation which, in the course of their celebration, elucidate themselves in a way that makes them clear to everyone, so that those present are addressed in the realm of their understanding and made aware of those elements in the celebration which apply to them personally (cf *Institutio Christianae Religionis* IV, 14, 4). On the other hand, he demands with emphasis that the celebration of a sacrament should open an "access to our hearts" so that the Christ who presents himself sacramentally in the power of his Spirit is able to penetrate "into the interior" of the one celebrating (cf *ibid.* IV, 14, 8). Here we have expressed a theology of the word which was peculiar to the Reformation and was made concrete by divine worship.

In a similar way, Vatican II recognizes the necessary analogical-digital structure of the sacraments in that it articulates the harmonious unity between "the awakening of the heart" and "the instruction of the mind," between an attitude of worship and a rational participation in the acts of the faith community (cf *SC* 21/2; 33/2). Here as well there occurs a union of a Christological approach with a theology of the word. And so we could say in view of the experience of Church history that the liturgy is in need of periodic revision (*liturgia semper reformanda*), that every derailment of sacramental practice in the direction of an over-emphasis on verbiage, prattle, intellectualizing teachiness, emotionalism, sectarian cultivation of self-importance and belongingness to the particular group can only be seen as an estrangement of its basic structure.

(d) A fourth aspect of an investigation of fundamental structures is the *sphere of freedom* which the expression of symbols affords. Without necessarily wanting to refer to Christian ritual celebration with the fashionable expression "non-controlled communication" (Habermas), we can interpret the urgent invitation of the Council to an "active participation" (*actuosa participatio*) in the sense that a free participation is intended. In fact, the Christian symbols of grace are structured according to the linguistic category "parable." Just as the parables of Jesus of Nazareth were *evocative* narratives (often with several possibilities of interpretation), designed to touch the hearers in their intellectual curiosity and to enable their free participation in the search for the reign of God, so also do the sacraments speak a kind of symbolic and parable-like language which intimates more than it clearly expresses, enabling the participants to *searchingly* react. Of course this refers to a searching of *faith* which is appealed to in its freedom and exercised in freedom. Because the Christian "signs of grace" are narrative, parable-like, symbolic, evocative, mystery-bearing linguistic figures, they can be referred to—already in this context—as *sacramenta fidei*. They create a sphere of freedom which enables an existentially active interpretation of God, Christ, faith-community, and the self—which is primarily a work of faith and a pre-condition to a faithful investment of one's self.

(e) Especially this fundamental character of the "sign" is particularly effective in those rites in which a *dialogue*, a conversation between those celebrating it, is possible. This can be the case primarily in the baptism and confirmation of adults, in the Eucharist, and in the sacrament of reconciliation. Here the sacramental play of language is essentially an alternating, a reciprocal delivering of messages, which is far from being a mere exchange of cognitive information. Here there occurs more of an interpersonal *encounter* when the psychological prerequisites (a clearly recognizable group, a minimum common denominator, practice in active liturgy, sufficient motivation) are safeguarded. Without doubt, these structural elements remain buried in many sacramental celebrations which are conducted all too much in the spirit of the old "feudal" understanding of the relationship between administrator and receiver. When a one-sided emphasis is placed on the authority of an official officeholder, resulting in an essentially monological style of communication, the structurally polyphonic communication of grace cannot unfold. In spite of this, the latter remains the desired goal of sacramental economy based on the essentially charismatic structure of the Pauline faith-community.

A renewed consciousness of this dialogical structure has commonly resulted in concrete practices such as improvised prayers of the faithful (which appropriately introduce the meal of thanksgiving in which unity is established between participants), dialogue-homilies, and conversational confessions (in which the priest and the penitent open themselves to each other), baptismal catechesis both before and/or after baptism (which is directed toward the concrete life-history of the individual and is more than a mere learning of a catechism). And could we not emphasize the dialogical as belonging to the basic structure of the progress of the "permanent sacraments" of matrimony and holy orders in their concrete life-history? Does the ability of marriage partners and of the full-time leaders of the faith-community *to hear and give answer* not bear sacramental character? And is not this the expression—in an especially lofty inter-personal form—of the fundamental linguistic character of the effective "signs of grace"?

(f) With this thought, that the experiential language of the sacraments is nothing other than the "imitation" of the designated "object" by the "sign" which designates it, we can appropriately end this first phase of our short analysis. According to a biblical understanding, the word of God, as well as that which is ritually represented and embodied, is an *effective word* of the Creator. Wherever God expresses himself, the substantial occurs. God's communications are never merely *verba volantia*, only acoustically relevant vocabulary. They are action-words and word-actions. They produce change and create the new. When the human celebrants of sacraments repeat words of God, or, better still, when they enter into a real *imitation* of the creative speaker, it becomes obvious to them that the entire liturgy, even purely psychologically and ethically, brings with it powers of change, renewal, and healing (cf Riess 147). This is at the same time true at the level of the dogmatic indicative as well as the ethical-existential imperative. The term "imitation" contains both: on the one hand, the believing knowledge of the activeness of God's spoken word which, even in borderline cases in which the human individual fails, maintains the effectiveness of its offer of salvation; on the other hand, the believing aspiration for an appropriately helpful, effective, inter-personal communication. Such an aspiration is all the more meaningful in that the encounter between God and man, as well as between human individuals, is exposed to many disturbances.

4.3.1.2. Disturbances

Inadequacies in the factual accomplishment of sacramental encounter can be of either an objective or a subjective nature. Objectively, communication is often thwarted by the medium itself, whether of the symbol or the word. In the development of cultural history, symbols can change and die. Once generally understood language can appear to later generations as puzzlingly strange language which then by no means any longer has the effect of the fascinatingly and attractively mysterious. Because the pre-conciliar communicative medium of the liturgy had lost, in many respects, both "analogical" and "digital" effectiveness, the Council introduced in this area a far-reaching reform. Whether the mere changing of the language of the sacraments from Latin to the various native languages has really effected a rejuvenation can be questioned in a number of respects. A basic tenet of communications theory was often forgotten, that every symbol is a symbol *for* someone—for a particular person, group, culture, and epoch—and that, as a result, after the disappearance of a particular addressee, that same symbol cannot without risk be employed to address new persons and groups. Religious *poetry* of the past, in which God is given the characteristics of a monarch enthroned over a court of angel choirs, or in which the experience of sin and guilt causes the faithful to make a perpetual *mea culpa* profession, does not necessarily represent the view of God or self or world held by people in an industrial age. And so the structural imperative arises automatically that new times demand new religious symbols and poetry. A "controlled growth" in this area would certainly overcome a number of communication's barriers in the celebration of sacraments. It is not possible in the long run to awaken a faith community to a lively exchange with dead symbols. Therefore again: *liturgia semper reformanda.*

Another "classical" disturbance in sacramental administration lies, so to speak, halfway between the objective and the subjective. Whenever those who are invited to the celebration are not *prepared* for this demanding group action, they can experience the celebration as a real chaos of symbols. The community leader who, because of stress or indifference, seeks to cover up his insufficient attention to the goal-group with a flood of platitudes; faithful who, without the least recollection, "pop into church" for Mass, a baptism, or a wedding; individuals who maintain the everyday climate of anonymity even during the celebration of ritual acts; workers and employers who are not able to divorce themselves from a mentality of class-struggle even in the ecclesial community: such and similar (to use Paul's terminology) *inappropriate* attitudes often contribute to an inauthentic, empty, boring, chaotic, and uncommunicative celebration. They produce an atmosphere that can smother any otherwise subjectively present desire for an encounter with God and one's fellow man. They form, so to speak, a practical *obex*, a group-psychological barrier to a communication of grace that aims at fullness and effectivity. And so, God himself is called upon to supply that "special effort" of which the Scholastics of the Middle Ages so ably spoke.

There are, of course, many examples of *impeded* communication for which it would be futile to look for any sort of fault in the participant. Very commonplace factors, such as lack of familiarity, insufficient education, diverse linguistic practice and sensibility, could make the celebration of a sacrament into a quite tortuous exercise. What science calls "meta-communication" can here be helpful. This consists in the "switching-over of a symbol-program, which is in progress and possibly obstructed, into another. In meta-communication it is possible to bypass, like an obstacle, blocked paths of communication" (Bastian 52). An example might be seen in a "celebrant" who makes an incidental remark in allusion to a totally non-liturgical circumstance, turns his attention playfully to one of the "communicants," interposes some personal work between two ritual statements, begins to sing a well-known song, or makes a surprising gesture within a solemn context.

Such playful skill at "switching over" is not only something which must be expected from a well-trained leader of the faith-community, but also from those celebrating with him in the self-confidence of their freedom (for they too can initiate meta-communication) and based on the demands of optimal practice. It also has to do with the theological essence of the sacraments as moments of encounter between the creative grace of God and the creative faith of the faithful. Where grace communicates itself, there is normally also a latently effective power of emancipation at work. Nothing corresponds better to the essential structure of divine self-communication as a playful, dancing "light-footedness" (cf Nietzsche's "dancing God") with which bogged-down, blocked channels of encounter are swept free again.

The *aggressions* that can arise in those present or participating in the celebration of a sacrament should not necessarily be interpreted as sacrilege. They are certainly not in every case a result of hatefulness or willing destructiveness. There are completely normal aggressions which arise from an unsatisfied desire to understand or a frustrated sensitivity for justice (see, e.g., the anger of Jesus in the temple). These have, if perhaps not a right to be "at home" in the sacramental process, at least a right to asylum there. This includes the "aggression" of criticism or self-criticism which has its prescribed place, for example, in the sacrament of penance or in the penitential rite introducing the eucharistic celebration. If, however, aggression becomes, after all, a malicious attack, the possibility is still given to redirect it through meta-communication.

Without doubt *sin*, the conscious and freely committed affront against God, presents for fellow men and for the faith-community the greatest disturbing factor for sacramental communication. This is not, in the first instance, the case at the level of the communication of grace, but primarily regarding the effectiveness of symbols. Insofar as sin consists essentially in the culpable absolutizing of individual self-interest, i.e., in egocentrism, it can be understood as an "impetus to broken relationships" (Jungel). Wherever such an impetus determines the overall relationship of human individuals (and does not lead to the exceptional case where a solidarity among accomplices develops), seen purely as group psychology, there is a communications disturbance present. This justifies, in part at least, the thematic emphasis which the liturgy places on the power of evil (possibly in remembrance of Jesus' "casting out demons").[7]

4.3.1.3. Faith Community

That the reponsibility for the sacraments lies with each concrete faith community is a fact that is structurally determinative. According to the understanding of the primitive Church, the community incorporated its members through baptism and the Lord's Supper. Following the concepts of communications theory, this is a group which "socializes" individuals into its midst through a complex system of interactions, i.e., produces a certain "we-consciousness."

Since most of the sacraments are received for the first time during childhood, the local assembly (usually the parish) stands in very close proximity to the *family* which can rightly be called "the first school of communication."[8]

Normally a more or less intensive cooperation arises between the family and the faith community in that process of "sacramentalization" in which the maturing individual learns determinative concepts, values, and patterns of behavior, in which he learns to play his necessarily multi-faceted role and to practice the art of overcoming conflict. This cooperative and integrated communicative schooling by the *ecclesia domestica* and the *ecclesia localis* assumes varying forms. It occurs, for example, in the post-baptismal catechesis which reaches its culmination in confirmation, the moment of conscious acceptance of one's "mission" in Church and society; here the psychological process of maturation and the development of faith-life toward maturity converge, whereby the family and the faith community each contributes in its own particular way. A further example of this would be the cooperative process of learning the skill of celebrating the Eucharist in its context of life, world, and society—whereby it is unimportant to determine from which "ecclesial sphere" the faithful learn to overcome their egocentricism and to participate in the Lord's Supper with a real willingness for communication. Only the fact itself is important that human individuals are made capable of a mentality in which a two-dimensional eucharistic *communio* is possible, as a sociologist of religion has appropriately described:

> "Two or three" meet each other in communion, whether they are man and wife, friend and friend, or friend and enemy, repulsive or strange, not because they belong together in life, but in spite of the fact that they do not belong together in life. Two or three meet each other in *his* name when they celebrate with him the death of their self-will.[9]

The faith community and the Christian family contribute optimally to a cooperative furthering of such practice only when the socialization process of society as a whole develops counter to that of the Church to a very minimal degree. Then only very few of those "discrepancies in values and roles" arise that the investigations of the sociologists of religion have uncovered among many Christians in modern industrial society.

The local faith community is called in any case to conduct the kind of enlightened and enlightening "sacramental didactic" that enables the individual Christian to get his feet on solid ground. This ground is then solid when the faith community is able to interpret the faith tradition, the creedal code and the sacramental language of its members in such a way that it is not estranged from the everyday experiences of their work, their recreation, or their politics, and that it enables them above all to see their responsibilities in these areas in a specifically Christian light. They will then be able to correlate and communicate with the worldliness of the world around them in the spirit of their faith. And they will not become victims of a religious-secular schizophrenia.

In this respect, the statements of the Council on the "inculturation" of the sacramental into the various lands of the earth is not without meaning. In the consciousness that the central mystery of faith in Christianity, in distinction to the mystery religions, is of revelatory and open character, the Council was insistent that the sacraments should finally speak the language that is native to each cultural area. It rejected a "rigid uniformity" and at the same time recognized the necessity to "respect and foster the qualities and talents of the various races and nations" in the celebration of the liturgy (SC 37; cf 40/2; AG 21/3). Wherever such a cultural exchange is present between the concrete faith community and the socio-cultural context that supports it, this ecclesial cell will—as well "within" its ritual expression—serve as a communicative context of the Church as *communio sanctorum*.

4.3.1.4. Life History

As was already indicated in the previous section, the structurally determining goal of the sacramental economy lies in the fact that sacraments constantly accompany the faithful in their very own personal life history. Or, as the Council formulates it: "Thus, for well-disposed members of the faithful, the liturgy of the sacraments and sacramentals[10] sanctifies almost every aspect of their lives with divine grace which flows from the paschal mystery of the passion, death and resurrection of Christ" (*SC* 61).

A similar thought led Thomas Aquinas to his systematizing the signs of grace according to seven intensive moments of "physical life" which concern both its personal and social "perfecting" (*STh* III 65, 1f). Rahner follows him in this with his discussion of the seven "situations of salvation" (*KuS* 85, 104). It need not be discussed here whether such a numerical systematizing of those determinative events, intensive moments, or situations of salvation in the life of a human individual is meaningful. The observation is sufficient that the modern science of communication is also aware of an existential "communications continuum" and that this continuum reaches from the "intra-uterine period" to "advanced age" (Riess 115f). It can be added that periods and moments of life that are indicated by such terms as early and later childhood, adolescence, school, friendship, first love, studies, trips, political activity, choice of profession or partner or residence, sickness, conflict, struggle, aging, approach of death, etc., can also be understood as focal points of human encounter which both change and confirm individual personalities. In such encounter, the individual functions sometimes as "sender," sometimes as "receiver," and sometimes as living "medium," especially in those incidences in which the personal life history stands in long-term relationship to another (e.g., marriage partner) or with several others (e.g., parents, children). The sacraments then, each with its own particular goal, are present for just this purpose, for *supporting* this continuum.

This idea is, according to Vatican II, based on the concept that every Christian participates in the *eschatological "pilgrimage"* of God's people. He is essentially "underway" toward a goal of perfection that, in the last analysis, God alone can give (cf *SC* 8). He moves from one level of communication to another in the protective fold of a people whose "destiny is the kingdom of God" (*LG* 9/2; cf 48/2; *GS* 45/1). He allows himself to be carried forward by the same growth-dynamic that is implicit in the coming reign of God. The sacraments offer him actual eschatological help in this respect in that they "prefigure" (*LG* 35/2) and anticipate already in the present that which belongs to the final consummation.

With this, the sacramental economy of exchange is enriched with a dimension in which one's "own personal" present communes with the promised future; "my" today lives from God's tomorrow. This means that the practice of the sacraments should proceed, never as a form of isolated "tactic" but always as a dynamic "strategy of the future." Progress as well as retrogression in the personal history of communication is to be interpreted in this conceptual context. An example would be sacramental reconciliation in which sins committed in the face of the infinite possibilities of a future which God himself has opened to us are not seen as tragedies but rather as ethical incentives to a new beginning.

Much could still be said about sacramental practice in this perspective of life history insofar as it constitutes the structure of the sacraments as the "celebration of symbols." But here one further thought can be hazarded—that God's word, insofar as it is specifically intended as word-deed *for* concrete human individuals and possesses real communicative character, cannot be indifferent to the ever relevant situation of the life-history of its "hearer." The revelation, as well as that which is sacramental, is an occurrence of relationships.[11] However, the receptive situation changes even in a most powerful continuum. There are high points and low points of our receptivity. In just this fact it can be seen that God's word is a *message* for the "just and unjust," for such as are prepared for it and such as are unprepared. It is good news or critical news, Gospel unto salvation or unto judgment. With this, we touch upon the second level of sacramental structure, the profound depths of grace.

4.3.2. The "Signified"

Because the reality which is signified by the sacraments is of a communicative nature, its symbols themselves must be understood as communication. The "sign" must be at the same level as "the signified," and its "language" must participate in the dynamic of the object to which it refers and of which it speaks. That was the thesis of which we spoke with hypothetical care.

It remains here only to present a more precisely developed proof of the concept which has already been referred to a number of times—that the sacramentally imparted reality has an essentially communicative structure. This can be done by referring to a few determinative New Testament texts, i.e., with only a necessary minimum of argumentation. This concerns that area which Scholastic theology summed up under the term "effectivity," and referred to more precisely as "grace," "sacramental grace," and in a few cases as "character" (which will not be treated here because of a lack of biblical references).

When the New Testament texts are consulted as to what baptism "effects" in the individual, a number of answers are given. The oldest texts refer to the healing and justifying of particular idolaters and similar pagan sinners "in the name of our Lord Jesus Christ" and "in the Spirit of our God" (1 Cor 6:11), or to the unifying of many very different individuals "into one body" through the "one Spirit" of their baptism (1 Cor 12:13), or to the foreordained and existential fellowship of the faithful with the crucified and risen Jesus Christ in which a freedom from sins and the ability to live "for God in Christ Jesus" (Rom 6:3-11) is given. In later texts, the forgiveness of sins and the gift of the Holy Spirit stand out as simultaneous effects of this rite of initiation, whereby, according to the context, it always refers to individuals who have opened themselves to faith (e.g., Acts 2:38; 22:16). Of course, definitive statements as to the relationship between this decision of faith on the part of the baptized and the saving gift of God, which he confers in sovereign freedom, are not to be found. Still, the overall testimony of the New Testament shows that the honest profession of faith in Jesus Christ (cf Mt 10:39), or the love which is of equal value (cf Lk 7:47), has the same effectiveness as baptism, that is, acceptance by God and freedom from the burden of sin. It is therefore all the more understandable that the basic predisposition of faith belongs organically to the "objective effectivity" of this rite of initiation.

The correlation between faith and salvation is extremely clear in the latest texts or fragments of tradition: "The man who believes... and accepts baptism will be saved" (Mk 16:16); the believers who have come to the faith through the proclamation of the Gospel enter into a relationship with the Father, the Son, and the Holy Spirit in whose name, i.e., into whose innermost mystery of existence, they are baptized (Mt 28:19); from the context of faith in the Son of God arises John's statement that those who are "begotten of water and Spirit" are those who "enter into God's kingdom" (Jn 3:5; cf 3:13-21).

What is the situation with the Lord's Supper whose "effectivity" is also formulated in a number of different ways? According to Paul, the "concern" of the Lord's Supper is the proclamation of the death of Jesus Christ "until he comes," and the contingent eschatological mobilization of the participants in brotherly love (1 Cor 11:26); or it consists in a "participation" (*koinonia*) in the body and blood of Christ, i.e., in the present reality of his totally self-sacrificing person (1 Cor 10:16f), a fact that makes of "the many" a single body. According to John, those who eat "the bread of heaven" in faith are given life, eternal life, and are promised resurrection; but the pinnacle of the gift is that they "remain" in Jesus and Jesus in them (Jn 6:51-57). The "concern" of Jesus' Supper is therefore totally one of *encounter*, or, better still, of "reciprocal immanence" (Schnackenburg), a mutual exchange in the life history of the partners in communication.

All of this picturesque and colorful testimony indicates clearly that the sacraments in this original form were not simply communicative events directed toward communion on the level of ritual celebration, as complexes of liturgical symbols and collective actions of the faith community. Not only formally but as well in substance they can be defined as communication, as *events of saving exchange between God and the faithful*. And that these events are to be understood in the sense of a creative economy that actually binds existence with existence, life history with life history, i.e., is to be understood quite "realistically," is shown by Paul's expressed use of the term *soma*. This term meant for the apostle more than just individuality. It expresses essentially—in the language of Kasemann—the "possibility of communication." As a *corporeal* being, the individual is oriented toward the other, "bound by the world, claimed by the Creator...in the possibility of concrete obedience and self-sacrifice."[12] As "corporeal being," more precisely as a physical being who is impregnated with the Holy Spirit, Christ presents himself for sacramental fellowship to the faithful now and always. As "body for us" (cf 1 Cor 11:24; in the original text: *to soma mou to uper umon*) he presents himself in baptism and Lord's Supper in order to incorporate the faithful into the communicative reality of his person. This incorporation into the universally open and receptive "body of Christ" occurs, of course, only then in its fullest form when the addressees themselves become open and receptive "bodies-for-Christ" and "bodies-for-each-other"; and this is only possible through a life determined and directed by faith. The effective goal of the sacramental encounter, then, is the ethically concrete mutual incorporation of the Christ, who is "for others," and his followers who, by grace, are enabled themselves to be "for others."

Systematic theology has reduced this rich biblical material to the simplified schema of *grace and faith* in which the reciprocal relationship of these two composed the "content" of the sacramental celebration. According to an approach using a theory of communication, however, this schema can only then be applied in a fruitful way when a very specific concept of grace and faith, which found little attention from the Scholastics, is incorporated into it.

Grace, then, should not be divided into a divine and a human dimension, into a "created" and an "uncreated" gift. Rather it must be conceived of as the self-communication of God with the purpose of making human self-realization possible. Grace is really God himself in his free, unearned, and never interrupted offer of himslf to human individuals; it is the freely given, anthropocentrically directed, effective apex of divine love. It is clear, then, that the "synthesis" of this divinity of God, which is so directed toward man, is to be seen in Jesus, the Christ.

Faith can be understood as the human counterpart of this free and creative relationship between God and man. The basic stance of faith consists as well in self-communication, self-presentation, and self-sacrifice. The believer opens himself to God, places his trust in him, and, in his personal development, turns toward God who comes to him in Christ. This act of faith can also be termed a "synthetic" act. Psychological observation alone gives an indication that faith seeks to hold together all of the various drives of the believer, and is able "to drive all competition from the field. His ability to organize the powers of emotion, will, and intellect, to keep the human system, individually or collectively and in spite of all disturbances, goal-oriented, is at the same time impressive and frightening" (Bastian 27).

The believer is then challenged by the sacraments in his total intellectuality as physical being to open himself to an *interactive* relationship with God. The entire symbolic language of sacramental celebration serves this purpose. This is not an abstract "grace in itself" over which the administrator could have control, but a personalized self-offer of God which is always directed concretely to human individuals, a self-offer which expects from the believer as a member of a particular faith-community an answer of faith and corresponding practical activity. The interaction, which is aimed at and is "suggested" by the divine Creator, will, of course, always be "asymmetrical" since the active part played by the human individual, in spite of the expansion of his possibilities through grace, cannot go beyond the limits of his own abilities. Still, this is nonetheless a real and free cooperation (*cooperari*) as it was stated by the Council of Trent (*NR* 795, 822; *DS* 1525, 1554). In this sense, the sacrament, at its very core, tends toward a characteristic communication between God and man which, in turn, becomes the medium for a many-faceted communication between human individuals. And so it is correct to say that the reality which is symbolized by the signs of grace has a communicative nature.

4.4. The Function of the Sacraments

Now that several aspects have been considered regarding the basic structure of the sacraments, a concluding attempt can be ventured to sum up what has already been said from the perspective of sacramental function. In this, the classical three-dimensional scheme of communications theory, sender-receiver-medium, will be employed, of course in a form which has been enriched by sacramental theology. This too is based on a point of emphasis set by Vatican II. The Council, in its statements concerning the "fundamental question," nowhere systematically followed the classical sequence of topics: effectivity, institution, number, necessity, administrator, communicant; rather, it placed the questions of the "minister" and of the "communicant," which were usually treated last, in the center of their considerations and repeatedly treated the question of the administrator-communicant-*relationship*.

How does a sacrament function? In what way can sacramental celebration also be described "technically" as occurrence of a communicative system? The answer which

will be sketched here should be understood as an attempted
answer and a contribution to further discussion. To do this,
an illustration will be employed as visual clarification.

The illustration consists of two triangles. They indicate
that in every sacramental celebration a double system of
communication is involved: on the one side are relationships brought about on the level of the symbol (*signum*), and
on the other side there are relationships indicating the
reality of the mystery symbolized (*res*). Both are directed
toward a single, specific addressee, the so-called *receiver*
(communicant) of the sacrament. Therefore this addressee is
placed at the upper point of the illustration which is the *point
of convergence* of both system-levels. That which is here
intended is at least partially reflected in the old Scholastic
principle: *"sacramenta pro hominibus"*—the sacraments
are intended totally *for* human individuals. They are the
goal at which the sacramental communication of grace and
the ritual, which conveys it, aim. Naturally, the communicant (receiver) does not occupy his place at the point of
convergence as an isolated individual. He is the member of
the faith community; he stands in the midst of the
concentrically structured Church of God which enfolds him
both as universal Church and as particular faith community, and ever—as in the case of marriage partnership and the
family which forms the "domestic church"—as small
"ecclesial" cell.

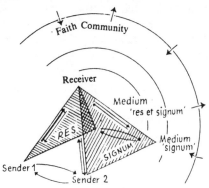

The *faith community* can be understood as a complex system of communication. It is a so-called open system, permeable to influences from within and from without, to suggestions, to socio-cultural conditions; but at the same time it is moved by powerful apostolic, evangelistic, critical, and dialogical impulses. It is a community "in the world and its environment." As such it brings with it the traditional components of its profession of faith, of the Creed and the language of faith, i.e., of the code that makes it possible, as well in sacramental liturgy, for sender and receiver to understand each other and to speak a common idiom. The faith community is responsible for the *media* in the narrowest sense. It sets the norm. It provides the necessary freedom for its creative development. As *matrix* of the sacramental media (the history of the Church gave birth to them), the faith community is the place where the old and the ever new flow into the functional development of sacramental celebration. The old Scholastic concept of causality appears to be little suited to making this dynamic process that marks the ecclesial transmission of grace to the communicant understandable. Today, cybernetic thought forms according to which the sacramental action is seen more adequately, not as a "one-way street" of cause and effect, but as a functionally mutual action, as a bundle of reciprocal effects, would appear to be more relevant. In fact, the faith community as matrix of the sacraments is dependent not only on the omnipotence of God, but also on neighboring systems, whether they are of a relevant-psychological or a permanent socio-cultural nature.

In the midst of this complex and dynamic system of the ecclesial milieu, the *minister* of sacraments is active. Without doubt, he stands in the service of the faith community, even when he appears to act alone. Strictly speaking, that is just the point, that he in reality never acts alone. Not as if he were a great sorcerer and administrator of mysterious powers, not as if he were the only fatherly point of personal reference for the sacramental communicants. According to the understanding of communications theory, he is the *catalyzer* of interactive points of reference. That means that he is a receptive sender and a sending receiver, as is indicated in the illustration by the arrows between the "receiver" (the permanent main addressee) and "sender." Not only the permanent sacraments of matrimony and holy orders present good examples of this in that they include an essentially dialogical life-style in which both sides are permanently engaged in sending and receiving; also the sacrament of penance can be mentioned in which, according to modern understanding, even the necessary "passing of sentence" is the cooperative result of an authentic dialogical exchange.

It cannot be emphasized strongly enough how much a modern feeling for life—and also, at least to a degree, the (otherwise so-called patriarchal) cult forms of the primitive and ancient Church—call for an *interactive partnership* wherever possible. Here it would appear that the research of sacramental theology has a broad field of investigation before it. The Council itself placed the accent on the "active participation" of *all the participants* and on a removal of all questionable passivity from the liturgy. For only based on such a "mutual obedience" can sacramental signs really function to simultaneously express and build community.

It has already been stated clearly that the "secondary minister" plays an especially important role in this through his own living testimony. This consists, at the least, in his attempt to be honest, not to contradict through his life-style what he really is. The administration of sacraments that does justice to faith and the communication of its grace has, in any case, catalyzing effect in this interaction of the partners. For in this, the "secondary minister" is optimally and operationally conformed to the "primary minister." It is clear, then, that this attestation of the "content" by the action of the mediator of grace himself is not exhausted only in piety, but demands as well acquired knowledge and a practical ability to communicate. Jesus also possessed communicative knowledge and ability (one needs only to think of his parables alongside his close inner solidarity with God and his correspondingly great kindness. In keeping with this behavioral norm, which is established by Jesus himself, a case of misbegotten, frustrated sacramental communication on the part of the minister (as well as of the communicant) must be considered the exception. In any case, the *ex opere operato* argument should not be misused as a theoretical-practical stopgap excuse.

The *medium* then is primarily (even if not totally) the responsibility of the minister, that is, the responsibility of his interactive relationship to the communicant and to the concrete faith community. The medium is above all the *signum*, the sign, the rite. It integrates through its appeal to the senses those elements which are both permanent and variable, traditionally stable and creatively devised. As such it can be understood as message, as essentially information directed toward the addressee and bearing real content. How this message of the "signum" itself bears the "res" is also demonstrated by the fact that in theological tradition its most pronounced equivalent is found in the so-called *res et signum* formula. This refers to that immediate (usually ecclesial) effect out of which then the further "results" or effects arise. In the case of the Eucharist, for example, this "inter-medium" is the fraternal fellowship of the banquet guests. It is at the same time the signified content and the signifying sign. It is signified by the communicative medium of the meal. And it significantly aims at the inner union of the communicant with Christ. It must be maintained that it is most highly characteristic for the structure of the Eucharist that the "inter-medium" of the "Christian fellowship" does not end with the realization of that "Christian fellowship" (as a worn-out vehicle), but rather it achieves in this fellowship its own greatest fulfillment.

In this, the pivotal point of sacramental communication becomes clear, namely the "primary minister" or (see the illustration) the *Sender 1*. This refers to God himself who has been once-for-all revealed in Christ and is creatively active through his Spirit. It is not possible here to consider the

Trinitarian structure of God's existence and activity, although it could very well provide a kind of primordial model of all communication. It must be sufficient to note that theological tradition signifies as the ultimate subject of sacramental acts sometimes God, sometimes Christ, and sometimes the Holy Spirit. It is of first importance to state here the basic perception of faith, that it is the *communicative nature of God* himself which makes the functioning of a sacramental economy possible and gives it permanent momentum.

God does not do this, of course, as if he were a blind "primary cause" which, according to the laws of mechanical necessity, set a chain of "secondary causes" in motion. Rather God "sends" as the primal sender in such a way that he aims at a very particular interaction (which is, naturally, "asymmetrical"). Because the receivers of his sacramental message are *free* individuals who are caught up in the process of becoming free, individuals with their own personal life-history, God offers himself in a willingness for dialogue, cooperation, and covenant. In baptism, this self-offer of God is concretized in that he calls the "receiver" to a participation in his "death, burial, and resurrection." In the Eucharist this occurs in such a way that Christ, the "sender," makes himself the "medium"; his body and his blood, i.e., his own self-sacrificial person, are offered as food for the ecclesial unity and fraternity. And he does this essentially *ex opere operato*, without unduly concerning himself with the worthiness or unworthiness of his guests. Since the formulation of the Pauline and Johannine theology of the Lord's Supper, however, it is clear that he expects, in this context, an interactive response.

In this respect, those *disturbances*, to which sacramental celebration is always subject, can be addressed. The communicative disturbance of *sin* can only be removed by "Sender 1," even when this occurs through the priestly medium of absolution. As well in the case of a possible *nihil* of apathy or of passivity, it is finally the Holy Spirit who is competent. However, with respect to obstructions on the level of the *signum,* and even of the *signum et res,* these are totally within the area of the responsibility of the faith-community, of the "co-receivers," and, in their midst, of the "Sender 2" whose competence in the area of *meta-communication* and reform contributes considerably to an overcoming of many linguistic barriers on the sacramental and cultural levels.

With this thought we bring to an end the present considerations. It certainly indicates that the communications-theoretical approach can only be applied with the proviso that one does not fall into the trap of a one-sided "technology" (which would perhaps be still less appropriate than a one-sided Aristotelianism). A sacrament can never be made real in the sense of a computer, a cybernetic automat, or an ably conducted group game. If communications theory is to be useful for a doctrine of sacraments, as we believe it to be, then it will be so only under the condition that everything is considered and formulated in a way *that does justice to the mystery.* By mystery is meant not only the mystery of God in Christ but also the mystery of the existential depths of groups and individuals for whom the sacraments of the Christian Church exist.

NOTES

Chapter One

1. Cf. G. Wagner, *Das religionsgeschichtliche Problem von Rom. 6:1-11* (Zurich, 1962).

2. Cf. as a typical example the so-called Nassener sermon in *Hipp Ref* V, 7ff, briefly described in Bornkamm, 818.

3. Cf. W. Wrede, *Das Messiasgeheimnis in den Evangelien* (Gottingen, 1901), 5ff, and R. Bultmann, *Die Geschichte der synoptischen Tradition* (Gottingen, 1931).

4. According to the Egyptian text where, in contrast to the Western text, the word *martyrion* (witness) appears in place of *mysterion*.

5. Cf. K. Rahner, art. "Apologeten," in *LThK* I, 721ff. For the concept of sacrament by the Church Fathers, cf. J. de Ghellinck, *Pour l'histoire du mot 'sacramentum,'* Vol. I (Loven, 1924).

6. H. von Soden, "Mysterion and sacramentum in den er zwei Jahrhunderten," in *ZNW* 12 (1911) 188-227.

7. Cf. A. Kolping, *Sacramentum Tertullianum* (Regensburg-Munster, 1948); and D. Michaelides, *Sacramentum chez Tertullien* (Paris, 1970).

8. Documentation by Michaelides, *op. cit.,* 23.

9. Cf. J. Huhn, *Die Bedeutung des Wortes Sacramentum bei dem Kirchenvater Ambrosius* (Fulda, 1929) 9f; O. Casel, "Zum Wort Sacramentum," in *Jahrbuch fur Liturgiewissenschaft* 8 (1928) 226ff.

10. Cf. O. Casel, "Das Mysteriengedachtnis der Messliturgie im Lichte der Tradition," in *Jahrbuch fur Liturgiewissenschaft* 6 (1926) 113ff, and "Neue Zeugnisse fur das Kultmysterium," in *op. cit.* 13 (1935) 109ff.

11. G. Anrich, *Das antike Mysterienwesen in seinem Einfluss auf das Christentum* (Tubingen, 1894) 155f.

12. Cf. *De vic Dei* X, 5; *PL* 41, 282: "Sacramentum, id est sacrum signum." And for the entire problem complex, cf. C.P. Mayer, "Philosophische Voraussetzungen und Implikationen in Augustins Lehre von den Sacramenta," in *Augustiana* 22 (1972) 53–79.

13. F. Schupp, *Glaube-Kultur-Symbol. Versuch einer kritischen Theorie sakramentaler Praxis* (Dusseldorf, 1974) 207.

14. Cf. *De Doctr. Christ.* I, 4, 8 and 35, 39; *PL* 34, 20f. For Augustine's hermeneutic, cf. C.P. Mayer, *Die Zeichen in der geistigen Entwicklung und in der Theologie Augustins, II. Teil: Die antimanichaische Epoche* (Wurzburg, 1974) 294–301.

15. Cf. F. Schupp, *op. cit.*, 108f.

16. Concerning these theologians cf. the various handbooks for the history of dogma and especially J.R. Geiselmann, *Die Abendmahlslehre an der Wende der christlichen Spatantike zum Fruhmittelalter* (Munchen, 1933); and *Die Eucharistie der Vorscholastik* (Paderborn, 1926).

17. *Sent.* IV, d 1, n 2; *PL* 192, 839: "sacramentum enim proprie dicitur, quod ita signum est gratiae dei, et invisibilis gratiae forma, ut ipsius imaginem gerat et causa existat."

18. B. Geyer, "Die Siebenzahl der Sakramente in ihrer historischen Entwicklung," in *Theologie und Glaube* 10 (Paderborn, 1918) 325–338.

19. For specifics cf. P.B. Garland, *The Definition of Sacrament according to Saint Thomas* (Ottawa, 1959).

20. Concerning Luther's opinion in this respect cf. *WA* 6, 572, 10f; in general cf. E. Roth, *Sakramente nach Luther* (Berlin, 1952).

21. Further by G. Schrenk, "Zwinglis Hauptmotiv in der Abendmahlslehre und das Neue Testament," in *Zwingliana* 5, 1930/2, 176–185; and E. Blanke, "Zwinglis Sakramentsanschauung," in *Theologische Blatter* 10 (Leipzig, 1931) 283–290.

22. *Institutio Christianae Religionis* IV, 14, 9. For the structure of sacraments by Calvin cf. A. Ganoczy, *Ecclesia ministrans. Ministering Church and Church Ministry by Calvin* (Freiburg-Basel-Wien, 1968) 75–94.

Chapter Two

1. Duns Scotus, *Oxon* IV, d 1, q 5; in the original edition of this book quoted in German from J. Auer, "Allgemeine Sakramentenlehre," in *Kleine Katholische Dogmatik*, published by J. Auer/J. Ratzinger, Vol. VI (Regensburg, 1971) 80.

2. O. Casel, *Das christliche Kultmysterium* (Regensburg, 1935) 102.

3. O. Casel, "Glaube, Gnosis und Mysterium," in *Jahrbuch der Liturgiewissenschaft* 15 (1941) 268.

4. Cf. B. Geyer, *op. cit.*, 325-338.

5. Cf. *LG* 8/2; 16/1; *OT* 16/6. And for the entire problem, cf. A. Ganoczy, "Ausser Gott kein Heil?" in *Lebendiges Zeugnis* 32 (1977/4) 55-66.

6. Pope Innocent III, in an instruction to the bishop of Arles in 1201, *NR* 526; *DS* 781.

7. In this context cf. A. Ganoczy, *Devenit chretien. Essai sur l'historicite de l'existence chretienne* (Paris, 1973); in English, *Becoming Christian* (New York, Ramsey, Toronto, 1976).

Chapter Three

1. Concerning this problem cf. W. Kasper (ed.), *Chistentum ohne Entscheidung, oder: Soll die Kirche Kinder taufen?* (Mainz, 1970).

2. Cf. *KuS* 78: "Being made a member of the Church is therefore 'sacramentum et res' of this sacrament of Christian initiation." This means that it is at the same time something which "is symbolized," i.e., "is effected," and which "symbolizes" i.e., "effects."

3. Cf. Ott 419, where the term baptism, based on later witnesses such as John 3:5, Titus 3:5, and Ephesians 5:26, is mentioned exclusively in connection with the word "rebirth" which strikes one as rather "mysterious."

4. Cf. R. Schnackenburg, *Das Heilsgeschehen bei der Taufe nach dem Apostel Paulus* (Munchen, 1950).

5. The text here makes reference to Augustine in *Ps. 32, Enarratio* II, 29; *PL* 299; cf. *UR* 22/1; *LG* 15/1.

6. See Ott, 433f; cf. M. Adler. *Taufe und Handauflegung* (Munchen, 1951).

7. Cyprian, *Ep.* 73, 9ff; 74, 5 and 7; *PL* 3, 1206, 1221f.

8. *Cat. Myst.* 3; *PG* 33, 1087ff; *ibid.*, 17, 24f; *PG* 33, 996.

9. For the controversy concerning the sacrament of confirmation see *Trierer Forum* (1971), 3; cf. G. Biemer, J. Muller, R. Zerfab, *Eingliederung in die Kirche* (Mainz, 1972).

10. Cf. H. Feld, "Das Verstandnis des Abendmahls," *Ertrage der Forschung*, Vol. 50 (Darmstadt, 1976) 124-131; see in particular the contributions of J. de Baciocchi, P. Schoonenberg, E. Schillebeeckx, J.P. de Jong, and J. Betz.

11. *Ibid.,* pp. 136-139; see as well the anthology by J. Hafer, K. Lehmann, W. Pannenberg, E. Schlink, *Evangelisch-katholische Abendmahlsgemeinschaft?* (Regensburg-Gottingen, 1971); and "Reform und Anerkennung kirchlicher Amter," a memorandum of the fellowship of university institutes of ecumenism (Munchen-Mainz, 1973).

12. Cf. E. Schweizer. "Abendmahl," *RGG* 1, 10f.

13. H. Feld, *op. cit.,* p. 57.

14. Cf. *Didache* 9, 4; Cyprian, *Ep.* 63, 13; *PL* 4, 395f; John Chrysostom, *1 Cor hom.* 24, 2; *PG* 61, 200f.

15. *In Joan tr.* 26, 13; *PL* 35, 1613; cf. Thomas, *STh* III 82, 2 ad 3. The Council of Trent mentions as well the motive of unity: *NR* 567, 570; *DS* 1635, 1638.

16. Cf. K. Rahner, A. Haufling, *Die vielen Messen und das eine Opfer,* 2nd ed. (Freiburg, 1966).

17. In reference to the entire problematic cf. T. Felthaut, *Die Kontroverse uber die Mysterienlehre* (Wanndorf, 1947).

18. Especially important is the work of J. Betz, *Die Eucharistie in der Zeit der griechischen Vater,* Vol. I/1 (Freiburg, 1955); Vol. II/1 (2nd edition, 1964).

19. Cf. K. Rahner, "Die Gegenwart Christi im Sakrament des Herrnmahls," *Schriften zur Theologie,* IV (Einsiedeln, 1960) 357-385; E. Schillebeeckx, *Die Eucharistische Gegenwart,* 2nd ed. (Dusseldorf, 1968); for the debate concerning "transignification" and "transfinalization" cf. the contributions of J. de Baciocchi, P. Schoonenberg, and L. Smits in H. Feld, *op. cit.,* XXVI, XXX; cf. pp. 128f.

20. See in this respect A. Ganoczy. "Wesen und Wandelbarkeit der Ortskirche," *ThQ,* 158, 1 (1978) 1-14.

21. *UR* 15/1; on the topic of concelebration see as well *PO* 7/1; for a definition of the "particular Church" in the context of the Eucharist see *CD* 11/1.

22. Cf. *ThEu* 25; A. Ganoczy. "Glaubwurdiges Feiern der Eucharistie als Sakrament des Glaubens und der Einheit," *Wort und Antwort,* 14 (1973) 14-19.

23. See the suggestions for further thought given by P. Schoonenberg in his contributions which are listed in *ThEu,* p. 177, footnote 26.

24. In this respect see the thorough research of M. Thurian, *Eucharistie. Einheit am Tisch des Herrn?* (Mainz-Stuttgart, 1963).

25. Cf. B. Welte's contributions to the discussion in: M.

Schmaus (ed.), *Aktuelle Fragen zur Eucharistie* (Munchen, 1960) 184-195; summarized in *ThEu*, pp. 189-193.

26. J. Betz, *op. cit.,* "Die Aktualprasenz der Person und des Heilswerkes Jesu im Abendmahl nach der vorephesinischen griechischen Patristik."

27. Cf. A. Ganoczy, "Glaubwurdiges Feiern der Eucharistie," *op. cit.,* footnote 22.

28. Cf. F. Schupp, *Glaube-Kultur-Symbol, Versuch einer kritischen Theorie sakramentaler Praxis* (Dusseldorf, 1974); especially IV, "Symbol und Aufklarung," pp. 258-287.

29. The first clear evidence of this is found in Cyprian (*De Lapsis* 29; *PL* 4, 503f); John Chrysostom (*De Sacerd.* III, 6; *PG* 48, 643f) and Ambrose (*De Poen.* I, 2, 7; *PL* 16, 488).

30. Cf. Cyprian, *Ep.* 18, 1; *PL* 4, 27; Synod of Elvira, can. 32; *PL* 84, 305.

31. Cf. H. Kung, *Die Kirche* (Freiburg-Basel-Wien, 1967); A. Greshake, "Zur Erneuerung des kirchlichen Busswesens," in A. Exeler *et al.* (eds.) *Zum Thema Busse und Bussfeier* (Stuttgart, 1971), 61-121.

32. Cf. Cyprian, *Ep.* 146, 1; *PL* 22, 1143f; *In ep. ad Tit.* 1, 5; *PL* 26, 555-598.

33. E. Schillebeeckx expresses himself in a similar vein in *ChSG* 59, 174f; criticism of this twofold division is expressed by F. Wulf in his commentary to *PO, LThK-K* III, 149ff.

34. In this respect see P. Lengsfeld, *Das Problem der Mischehe* (Freiburg-Basel-Wien, 1970) 140-148; R. Schnackenburg. "Die Ehe nach der Weisung Jesu und dem Verstandnis der Urkirche," in F. Henrich, V. Eid (eds.), *Ehe und Ehescheidung. Diskussion unter Christen* (Munchen, 1972); and J. Ratzinger. "Zur Frage der Unaufloslichkeit der Ehe," in *ibid.*

35. In this respect see E. Wilkens (ed.), *Ehe und Ehescheidung.* (Studienbucher Nr. 30) Hamburg, 1963; F. Henrich, V. Eid (eds.), *op. cit.*

36. Cf. *GS* 49/2; for the question of "mutuality" see *GS* 49/1— 50/3; *LG* 11/2; 35/3; 41/5.

Chapter Four

1. Cf. W. Oepke. *"Mesites," ThWNT* IV, 602-629.

2. Concerning the use by the Council of a *communio*-vocabulary I am preparing a separate treatise.

3. Concerning the concept of the "locality of human existence"

cf. my article "Wesen und Wandelbarkeit der Ortskirche," *ThQ* 158, 1 (1978) 1-14.

4. See in this respect the following works: R. Riess. "Orienttierung, Analysen, Alternativen," *Seelsorge* (Gottingen, 1973), 102-152 (especially 117-120); H.-D. Bastian, "Wie christlicher Glaube funktioniert," *Kommunikation* (Stuttgart-Berlin, 1972), esp. pp. 123ff.

5. Cf. Bastian, *ibid.*, p. 63.

6. See in this respect M. Jossettis, *Praxis des Evangeliums zwischen Politik und Religion. Grundprobleme der praktischen Theologie.* Chapter 7: "Kommunikation in Gottesdienst. Lerner oder Trosten?" (Munchen, 1974) 164-187; cf. Bastian, *op. cit.*, pp. 80ff.

7. For the problematic concerning "the loss of communication through sin" see Riess, *op. cit.*, pp. 147f; W. Pannenberg. *Was ist der Mensch? Die Anthropologie der Gegenwart im Lichte der Theologie* (Gottingen, 1962) 40ff.

8. J.L. Aranguren, *Soziologie der Kommunikation* (Munchen, 1967) 161.

9. E. Rosenstock-Huessy, *Soziologie* II (Stuttgart, 1958) 290ff.

10. The sacramentals are ritual acts (e.g., prayers, blessings, use of blessed objects) that demonstrate a certain structural similarity with the actual sacraments. Cf. Ott, 417f.

11. Regarding a "relational" concept of revelation cf. P. Tillich, *Systematische Theologie*, Vol. I, 3rd ed. (Stuttgart, 1956) 129-189; cf. Bastian, *op. cit.*, pp. 132f, 134f.

12. "Anliegen und Eigenart der paulinischen Abendmahlslehre," *Exegetische Versuche und Besinnungen*, Vol. I (Gottingen, 1965) 32ff.

BIBLIOGRAPHY

Adler, N. *Taufe und Handauflegung.* Munchen, 1951.

Anrich, G. *Das antike Mysterienwesen in seinem Einfluss auf das Christentum.* Tubingen, 1894.

Aranguren, J.L. *Soziologie der Kommunikation.* Munchen, 1967.

Bastian, H.-D. *Kommunikation. Wie christlicher Glaube funktioniert.* Stuttgart-Berlin, 1972.

Betz, J. *Die Eucharistie in der Zeit der griechischen Vater.* Vol. I/1, 1955; vol. II/1 (2nd ed.) 1964. Freiburg.

Biemer, G., Muller, J., Zerfass, R. *Eingliederung in die Kirche.* Mainz, 1972.

Blank, F. "Zwinglis Sakramentsanschauung," *Theologische Blatter.* (Vol. 10) Leipzig, 1931. pp. 283–290.

Bornkamm, G. *"mysterion" ThWNT* IV, 810ff.

Bultmann, R. *Die Geschichte der synoptischen Tradition.* (2nd ed.) Gottingen, 1931.

Calvin, J. *Institutio Christianae Religionis* IV.

Casel, O. *Das christliche Kultmysterium.* Regensburg, 1935. (2nd ed.) p. 102.

——. "Glaube, Gnosis und Mysterium," *Jahrbuch der Liturgiewissenschaft,* vol. 15, 1941, p. 268.

——. "Das Mysteriengedachtnis der Messliturgie im Lichte der Tradition," *Jahrbuch fur Liturgiewissenschaft,* vol. 6, 1926, pp. 113ff.

——. "Zum Wort Sacramentum," *Jahrbuch fur Liturgiewissenschaft,* vol. 8, 1928, pp. 226ff.

——. "Neue Zeugnisse fur das Kultmysterium," *Jahrbuch fur Liturgiewissenschaft,* vol. 13, 1935, pp. 109ff.

Denzinger, H. Schonmetzer, A. *Enchiridion Symbolorum.* (36th ed.) Barcinone-Freiburg, 1976.

190   *An Introduction to Catholic Sacramental Theology*

Feld, H. *Das Verstandnis des Abendmahls.* Ertrage der Forschung, vol. 50. Darmstadt, 1976.

Filthaut, T. *Die Kontroverse uber die Mysterienlehre.* Warendorf, 1947.

Ganoczy, A. "Ausser Gott kein Heil?", *Lebendiges Zeugnis,* vol. 32, 1977, no. 4, pp. 55-66.

——. *Devenir chretien. Essai sur l'historicite de l'existence chretienne.* Paris, 1973; English: *Becoming Christian.* New York-Ramsey-Toronto, 1976.

——. *Ecclesia ministrans. Dienende Kirche und kirchlicher Dienst bei Calvin.* Freiburg-Basel-Wien, 1968.

——. "Glaubwurdiges Feiern der Eucharistie," *GuL,* vol. 45, 1972, pp. 98-110.

——. "Die Eucharistie als Sakrament des Glaubens und der Einheit," *Wort und Antwort,* vol. 14, 1973, pp. 14-19.

——. "Wesen und Wandelbarkeit der Ortskirche," *ThQ,* vol. 158, no. 1, pp. 1-14.

Geiselmann, J.R. *Die Abendsmahrslehre an der Wende der christlichen Spatantike zum Fruhmittelalter.* Munchen, 1933.

——. *Die Eucharistie der Vorscholastik.* Paderborn, 1926.

Gerken, A. *Theologie der Eucharistie.* Munchen, 1973.

Geyer, B. "Die Siebenzahl der Sakramente in ihrer historischen Entwicklung," *Theologie und Glaube,* vol. 10, Paderborn, 1918, p. 325-338.

Ghellinck, J. de. *Pour l'histoire du mot "sacramentum."* vol. I. Loven, 1924.

Greshake, G. "Zur Erneuerung des kirchlichen Busswesens," Exeler, A., et. al. (eds.). *Zum Thema Busse und Bussfeier.* Stuttgart, 1971, pp. 61-121.

Henrich, F., Eid, V. (eds.). *Ehe und Ehescheidung. Diskussion unter Christen.* Munchen, 1972.

Hofer, J., Lehmann, K., Pannenberg, W., Schlink, E. *Evangelisch-katholische Abendmahlsgemeinschaft?* Regensburg-Gottingen, 1971.

Huhn, J. *Die Bedeutung des Wortes Sacramentum bei dem Kirchenvater Ambrosius.* Fulda, 1928.

Josuttis, M. *Praxis des Evangeliums zwischen Politik und Religion. Grundprobleme der Praktischen Theologie.* Munchen, 1947.

Kasemann, E. "Anliegen und Eigenart der paulinischen Abendmahlslehre," *Exegetische Versuche und Besinnungen,* vol. I. Gottingen, 1965 (4th ed.).

Kasper, W. (ed.) *Christentum ohne Entscheidung, oder: soll die Kirche Kinder taufen?* Mainz, 1970.

Kolping, A. *Sacramentum Tertullianum.* Regensburg-Munster, 1948.

Kung, H. *Die Kirche.* Freiburg-Basel-Wien, 1967.

Lengfeld, P. *Das Problem Mischehe.* Frieburg-Basel-Wien, 1970.

Mayer, C.P. "Philosophische Voraussetzungen und Implicationen in Augustins Lehre von den Sacramenta," *Augustiana*, vol. 22, 1972, pp. 53-79.

____. *Die Zeichen in der geistigen Entwicklung und in der Theologie Augustins, II. Teil: Die Antimanichaische Epoche.* Wurzburg, 1974.

Michaelides, D. *Sacramentum chez Tertullien.* Paris, 1970.

Neuner, J., Roos, H. *Der Glaube der Kirche in den Urkunden der Lehrverkundigung.* Regensburg, 1971 (9th ed.).

Oepke, W. "*Mesites,*" *ThWNT* IV, pp. 602-629.

Ott, L. *Grundriss der katholischen Dogmatik.* Freiburg, 1957 (3rd ed.).

Pannenburg, W. *Was ist der Mensch? Die Anthropologie der Gegenwart im Lichte der Theologie.* Gottingen, 1962.

Rahner, H. "Apologeten," *LTHK* 1, pp. 721ff.

Rahner, K. "Die Gegenwart Christi im Sakrament des Herrenmahles," *Schriften zur Theologie*, vol. IV. Einsiedeln, 1960, pp. 357-385.

____. *Kirche und Sakramente* (QD 10). Freiburg-Basel-Wien, 1960.

Rahner, K., Haussling, A. *Die vielen Messen und das eine Opfer.* Freiburg, 1966 (2nd ed.).

Riess, R. *Seelsorge, Orientierung, Analysen, Alternativen.* Gottingen, 1973.

Rosenstock-Huessy, E. *Soziologie II.* Stuttgart, 1958.

Roth, E. *Sakramente nach Luther.* Berlin, 1952.

Schillebeeckx, E. *Christus, Sakrament der Gottesbegegnung.* Mainz, 1960.

____. *Die Eucharistische Gegenwart.* Dusseldorf, 1968.

Schnackenburg, R. *Das Heilsgeschehen bei der Taufe nach dem Apostel Paulus.* Munchen, 1950.

Schrenk, G. "Zwinglis Hauptmotiv in der Abendmahlslehre und das Neue Testament," *Zwingliana*, vol. 5, 1930, no. 2, pp. 176-185.

Schupp, F. *Glaube-Kultur-Symbol, Versuch einer kritischen Theorie sakramentaler Praxis.* Dusseldorf, 1974.

Schweizer, E. "Abendmahl," *RGG* 1, pp. 10f.

Soden, H. von. "Mysterion und Sacramentum in den ersten zwei Jahrhunderten," *ZNW* 12, 1911, pp. 188-227.

Thurian, M. *Eucharistie. Einheit am Tisch des Herrn?* Mainz-Stuttgart, 1963.

Tillich, P. *Systematische Theologie,* vol. I. Stuttgart, 1956 (3rd ed.), pp. 129-189.

Wagner, G. *Das religionsgeschichtliche Problem von Romer 6, 1-11.* Zurich, 1962.

Welte, B. "Diskussionsbeitrage," *Aktuelle Fragen zur Eucharistie* (ed. by M. Schmaus). Munchen, 1960, pp. 184-195.

Wilkens, E. (ed.) *Ehe und Ehescheidung. Ein Symposion.* Hamburg, 1963. (Stundenbucher No. 30).

Wrede, W. *Das Messiasgeheimnis in den Evangelien.* Gottingen, 1901.

Zerfass, R. "Zum Streit um das Firmsakrament," *Trierer Forum,* vol. 7, 1971.